ENGLISH LITERATURE:
A PORTRAIT GALLERY

By the same Author

ENGLISH LITERATURE

A Portrait Gallery

BY

OLIVER WARNER

1964

CHATTO & WINDUS

LONDON

Published by
Chatto and Windus Ltd
42 William IV Street
London W.C.2

*

Clarke, Irwin and Co Ltd
Toronto

Printed in France by
Intergraphic Ltd

To Elizabeth

CONTENTS

vii

ERRATA

p. 16, line 21 For 'eclogues' read 'eclogues'
p. 20, line 14 For '1611' read '1616'
p. 32, line 8 For 'rhyme' read 'rhythm'
p. 38, line 8 For 'did nor' read 'did, or'
p. 68, line 15 For 'be' read 'by'
p. 72, line 3 For 'breath' read 'breadth'
p. 82, line 20 For 'Edmond' read 'Edmund'
p. 132, line 2 For 'an' read 'and'
    lines 1, 10, 13/14 and 21 For 'Fitzgerald' read 'FitzGerald'
p. 136, line 6 For 'Fitzgerald' read 'FitzGerald'
p. 168, line 23 For *The Ambassador* read *The Ambassadors*
p. 198, line 16 For 'those' read 'these'
    line 20 For 'Edward' read 'Edmund'

NOTE: In addition to those specifically acknowledged in the Foreword, thanks are tendered to the following for their kindness in according permission to reproduce items included in this series: the Librarian, Windsor Castle, on behalf of Her Majesty the Queen; Bodley's Librarian; the Trustees of the British Museum; the Curator, Farnham Museum; the Director, the Fitzwilliam Museum; the Hon. Mrs Clive Pearson; the Master and Fellows of Pembroke College, Cambridge; the Curator, the Maidstone Museums; the Trustees of the Tate Gallery; the Director, the Victoria and Albert Museum; and the Librarian of Winchester College, who went to much trouble in the case of William Collins.

FOREWORD

THE aim of this book is to enhance the pleasure of English literature by presenting a portrait gallery of some of its most illustrious men and women. The living have been excluded, since any choice would have been invidious.

Although few of the greatest are absent, practical considerations have dictated a limit of a hundred, the Brontë sisters being commemorated as one, in the well known combined portrait by their brother. There are, in the nature of the case, perceptible gaps, since a comprehensive roll of those who have lasting interest in letters would indeed be substantial. The compilers of the Authorised Version of the Bible are notable absentees, sponsors though they were of the most influential book in the language, and although it would have been possible to include William Tyndale, to whom James the First's translators owed so much, the real identity of the character who passes under Tyndale's name in a well-known portrait is, so experts believe, uncertain.

Steele, Gay, Landor, Pater and a number of philosophers are among the omissions, and most readers will sigh for a favourite or two of their own, perhaps Wycherley, or Clare. Moreover there is another group, which includes Malory, Marlowe, Webster and Vaughan the Silurist, who do not figure because no authenticated portrait exists. Even in the cases of Skelton, Herrick, Herbert, Defoe, Fielding and one or two others, something less than a fully satisfactory rendering has had to suffice, though in these instances, and in a very few others where identity is not irrefutably certain, a good history lies behind the picture. On the other hand, where the choice is wide, as sometimes happens, the quality of a work purely as a representation has been attended to, and there are instances in the nineteenth and twentieth centuries where, for this reason, or for lack of a superior portrait, a photograph has been preferred.

In the text, the attempt has been made to compress within a single page, lying opposite the portrait, the broad outline of the subject's life, and to suggest the chief reason for fame. The difficulties of such a survey are formidable and the drawbacks to concision, among them over-simplification, become evident soon enough: nevertheless the skill of a succession of artists, and the sheer interest of the people described will, perhaps, provide the necessary impetus, and at the same time offer a source of useful reference material.

The subtleties as well as the acerbities of literary criticism are absent, for in a gallery, given adequate labels and a respectable minimum of guidance, it is the pictures which provide the feast. It must therefore be a matter for regret that in a number of cases, particularly in the earlier years, the identity of the artists is unknown or at best uncertain.

The material itself is engrossing; the wealth of creative endeavour is beyond the grasp of a lifetime. Moreover, the close personal relationship between individual writers and groups of writers becomes in itself a quest, never more absorbing than in the instances of Sidney, Ben Jonson, Marvell, Pope, Samuel Johnson, Coleridge and Lamb. Later conditions have not always tended to encourage the close-knit group, but even now the isolated writer is comparatively rare.

In the pageant of letters, Tudor exuberance and experiment lead on to the splendour of Jacobean and Caroline verse and prose, and this to the luminous clarity of the eighteenth century. The age of reason gives place to the Romantics, the greatest of whom survives to take part in the diversified activity of the Victorians; and subjects select themselves. Then, with the age just past, perspective becomes uncertain; the difficulty of choice, the need for proportion becomes ever more acute. How is strictly relative merit to be assessed when the impact of a personality is still so fresh?

A high proportion of the portraits are drawn from the resources of the National Portrait Gallery, and the Scottish National Portrait Gallery, depositories for so much that is best in its field. Thanks are due, and are most warmly tendered, to the authorities of these and other collections whose help has been sought. The source in each case is given in the list of contents, and the artists are included in the index.

Great kindness and encouragement has been received from former colleagues serving in the Photographic Library and in the Publications Department of the British Council. Wherever this work may fall short, blame must be put squarely where it belongs.

ENGLISH LITERATURE
A PORTRAIT GALLERY

GEOFFREY CHAUCER

GEOFFREY CHAUCER, the first major poet in the English succession, was, even as a private citizen, an important, much travelled, much regarded man. As a youth he served under Edward III in France, and was there taken prisoner. Later he held various Court posts, and he was sent on missions to Genoa, to Florence (where he may have met Petrarch and Boccaccio), to Lombardy and Flanders. In due time he became Controller of Customs at the port of London, with a house over Aldgate and a wife who was sister-in-law to John of Gaunt, the son of Edward III and the ancestor of many kings. The poet became Knight of the Shire for Kent in 1386, and went on pilgrimage to Canterbury two years later. He died, full of honour, in 1400, and was buried in Westminster Abbey, a monument being placed there a century and a half later, when he was still without a peer within the realm of English poetry.

'O reverend Chaucere, rose of rethoris all . . .' – so wrote William Dunbar in *The Goldyn Targe*, a century after Chaucer's death, 'rethoris' alluding to his persuasion, grace and measure. Posterity agrees with the verdict, and the *Canterbury Tales*, first printed by William Caxton in 1478, have delighted mankind for five centuries with their affectionate description of human behaviour.

There is a full-page miniature of Chaucer reading his *Troilus and Criseyde*, in the library of Corpus Christi College, Cambridge, but the best-known portrait was made by Thomas Occleve (?1370-?1450) in the margin of one of his own works, now in the British Museum. Occleve's sketch is the basis of the panel illustrated.

SKELTON had the distinction of being created 'poet-laureate' by the ancient Universities of Oxford and Cambridge. He became tutor to Prince Henry, later King Henry VIII, and at one time enjoyed Court favour, despite a freedom as apparent in his poetry as in his life. He was admitted to Holy Orders before his pupil's accession to the throne, and was given the living of Diss, in Norfolk. He used to describe himself, without much charity to his parishioners, as Rector of Hell.

Modesty was not among Skelton's attributes and in *A Goodly Garlande of Laurell*, which appeared in 1523, a wood-cut represents his apotheosis. 'While the stars shine with eternal day,' runs the Latin inscription, 'and while the seas swell, there our laurels shall be green; this illustrious name shall be translated to the stars and everywhere shall Skelton be regarded as another Adonis.' In later life Skelton became critical of Wolsey, and as the result of his attacks he was forced to take sanctuary at Westminster, where he died not long before the disgrace of the Cardinal.

Skelton's most vigorous and popular poem was 'The Tunning of Elynour Rumming', Elynour was an ale-wife who brewed for 'travellers and tynkers, for sweters and swynkers, and all good ale drynkers'. As a description of the boisterousness of his times, this work is unequalled.

¶Skelton Poeta.

Eterno mansura die dum sidera fulgent
Equora dumq; tument hec laurea nostra virebit.
Hinc nostrum celebre et nomé referetur ad astra.
Vndiq; Skeltonis memorabitur altera a donis

SIR THOMAS MORE

'THE King's loyal servant: but God's first.' In these words More, with shrewd concision, summed up his life, and, moreover, gave the reason for his martyrdom at the hands of Henry VIII, a sovereign who had loved him, as all men did, but who designed to carry royal supremacy in church affairs beyond what was acceptable to More's conscience.

The son of a judge, More was brought up in the household of Cardinal Morton, and he practised the law with brilliant success. *Utopia*, his best-known literary work, was published at Louvain in 1516, Erasmus supervising the printing of the Latin text. An English version appeared some sixteen years after the author's death, and as its point was to discuss the ideal form of government, it proved immensely popular in a speculative age, and it has retained its interest and vitality.

After Henry VIII had repudiated the Pope's supremacy, More, who had succeeded Wolsey as Lord Chancellor, but then retired into private life, refused to take any oath which would impugn the authority of Rome or assume the justice of the King's divorce from his first Queen, Catherine of Aragon. His fate was inevitable. He was charged with high treason, found guilty, and beheaded.

More was a patron of Hans Holbein the Younger (1497-1543) who is said to have stayed three years at his Chelsea home. Through Holbein's skill, More is well commemorated.

Tho: Moor L Chancelour

Reproduced by gracious permission of Her Majesty the Queen

THOMAS WYATT, like his father before him, was a public servant of some eminence. After an educatioon at St John's College, Cambridge, he was employed by Henry VIII on diplomatic missions abroad. There he studied Italian verse, particularly the sonnet form, which he introduced and helped to popularise in his own country.

Wyatt was an admirer of Anne Boleyn, and he was confined to the Tower at the time of that Queen's disgrace. He recovered favour, and was again sent abroad on the King's business, being given an appointment with a delegation to the Emperor Charles V. After the fall of Thomas Cromwell, Wolsey's supplanter, Wyatt, who belonged to Cromwell's party, again found himself in trouble, but the defence which he wrote while in prison was so eloquent that he was freed. His respite was short. As his skill in languages and his experience in diplomacy were outstanding, he was commissioned in 1542 to meet the Spanish Ambassador at Falmouth and to convey him to London. On the way he caught a chill, and from the results of this he died in the fullness of life.

Wyatt's version of a number of the Psalms was published in 1549, seven years after his death. His original work was first collected in Richard Tottel's *Miscellany*, an anthology published in 1557 with nearly a hundred items by Wyatt, including rondeaux, lyrics, and satires in heroic couplets. Many of his lyrics were written for the lute; but in one or two he foreshadowed the colloquial and dramatic manner of Donne. Like Sir Thomas More, the poet had the good fortune to be drawn by Holbein.

Tho: Wiatt Knight.

Reproduced by gracious permission of Her Majesty the Queen

SURREY shared many attributes with Wyatt, with whom his name is linked, and like Wyatt he died young. The son of Thomas Howard, afterwards third Duke of Norfolk, he was bred to the Court, being cup-bearer to Henry VIII, ewerer at his Coronation, and Earl Marshal at the trial of Anne Boleyn. Henry's fifth Queen, Catherine Howard, was his cousin, and like Anne before her, she suffered execution. Surrey did not long survive the trial. After a life which included much fighting in Scotland and elsewhere, and constant brawls at home, he became victim to Henry's unreasoning jealousy. He was condemned and executed on frivolous charges, including treasonably quartering the royal arms, conspiring against the succession of Edward VI, and advising his sister to become the King's mistress.

Surrey favoured the sonnet form, as Wyatt did, and his work was also drawn upon by Tottel for his *Miscellany*, which included forty of his poems. He had the further merit of introducing, in translations from Virgil, the use of flexible blank verse, and he followed Wyatt in attempting versions of the Psalms, as well as paraphrasing part of Ecclesiastes. It was Surrey who wrote, on hearing of his friend's death five years before his own:

'Wyatt resteth here, that quick could never rest . . .'
Surrey's portrait, by Guillim Scrots (*fl.* 1546-1556), a Netherlands artist, is, like the verse, a gracious memorial to a short and crowded life.

SAT
SVPER
EST

SIR WALTER RALEGH

SPLENDID in his aims, ambitions and achievement, Ralegh carried Elizabethan attributes into the more sombre age of the Queen's successor. His end on the scaffold was tragic, yet it had the grandeur which belonged to the rest of his life. The portrait shows him in his magnificence, and although the artist is unknown, his skill is evident.

Born in South Devon, Ralegh went to Oriel College, Oxford, where he greatly distinguished himself. He began a career of adventure by soldiering abroad; pioneered voyages of western discovery; fought the Irish, and won the favour of Queen Elizabeth. Enemies and rivals soon endangered him, and by his secret marriage in 1593 to Elizabeth Throgmorton, a most enduring one, he temporarily lost royal favour.

Achievement restored it. Ralegh served with valour at Cadiz and the Azores, but in the end his very success against the Spaniards helped in his undoing. After the Queen's death in 1603, James I was for peace. Ralegh found himself in the Tower, from which he emerged, too late in life, to head an expedition to Guiana. Failure meant extinction, and the King did not spare him.

Ralegh's *History of the World*, wonderful in its comprehension, was never completed, but it enshrines much of his ripe experience in peace and war. His longest poem, *Cynthia*, is also incomplete, but his lyrics are memorable and his prose includes a masterpiece of geographical speculation and adventure, *The Discoverie of the Empyre of Guiana* (1596).

?1552-1599

In an age starred with great poets, Edmund Spenser stands among the greatest, honoured for his long poem *The Faerie Queen* and for those shorter works in which *Prothalamion* and *Epithalamion* are pre-eminent.

A Londoner by birth, Spenser was sent to Merchant Taylor's School and afterwards to Pembroke Hall (now Pembroke College), Cambridge, where hangs the best of various portraits, by an unknown hand. His principal work, parts of which are lost, was begun in 1579. He used in it a stanza of eight five-foot iambic lines, followed by a ninth of six feet, which he not only invented, but handled with great dexterity, sometimes with magic effect. In the same year he published his pastoral *The Shepheards Calendar* which was widely praised.

The Faerie Queen signified Glory in the abstract and Queen Elizabeth in particular. Long before the appearance in 1596 of the sixth of the surviving books, Spenser was established in public favour – he was given Kilcolman Castle in Ireland, a country about which he wrote much both in prose and verse – and had general recognition among men of letters.

In 1598 the Irish, led by the Earl of Desmond, rose and burnt Kilcolman, which had once been Desmond property, Spenser being forced to fly for refuge to Cork with his wife and four children. He died the following year in London and was buried at Westminster Abbey near his favourite Chaucer. It is probable that substantial fragments of the *Faerie Queen* perished in the flames of Spenser's home, but abundance survives to establish it as one of the representative poems of its age. It is richly allusive, and although the key to some of its inner meaning is lost, its mood is marvellously sustained.

ALTHOUGH he died of wounds received in action at the age of thirty-two, Sir Philip Sidney left a reputation in literature and in other fields which would have been remarkable in a far longer life. Born in 1554 and educated at Shrewsbury and Christ Church, Oxford, Sidney travelled in Europe, where he met Tintoretto and Veronese, and in 1583 married Frances, daughter of the statesman Sir Francis Walsingham.

Sidney, who was a member of the Areopagus, a club formed chiefly for the purpose of naturalising the classical metres in English verse, was on familiar terms with the leading writers of his day, and Spenser dedicated his *Shepheard's Calender* to him. His own work, though circulated during his lifetime, remained unprinted until after his death at Zutphen in 1586, where he was in service under Prince Maurice of Nassau against the Spaniards. As he lay stricken on the field, he passed a cup of water to another wounded man, saying: 'Thy necessity is greater than mine'.

Sidney's writing includes *Arcadia*, a prose romance interspersed with pastoral ecloques; a sonnet series, *Astrophel and Stella*; and *The Apologie for Poetrie* probably written at Wilton in 1580. A methodical examination of the poet's art, the *Apologie* embodies a discussion of the state of verse then current, and this was of a kind which had not before appeared in English.

An unknown artist painted Sidney in about 1577 in the resplendent clothing favoured by aristocrats of his time.

BUILDING up his reputation by means of the law, in which profession he rose, by successive steps under Queen Elizabeth and King James I, to become Lord Chancellor, Bacon hoped to win immortality through the variety and content of his writing. Much of his work was composed in Latin, owing to his belief in the universality and permanence of that language.

Bacon remarked that the way to power was by a winding stair. His own life proved the truth of that observation. The friend of Queen Elizabeth's favourite, the Earl of Essex, he had a large share in Essex's overthrow for treasonable conspiracy. Twenty years later he was himself in straits. He was charged before the House of Lords with bribery, deprived of his offices, fined, condemned to arrest during the King's pleasure, and disabled from sitting in Parliament. His last years were spent not in prison but in retirement, of which he made good use by literary pursuits.

In fact, most of his best work had already been done – his *Advancement of Learning*, published in English in 1605; his *Novum Organum*, a philosophical treatise which appeared in Latin the year before his impeachment, and above all his *Essays*, the first edition of which, that of 1597, contained ten examples. The second, which appeared in 1612, was expanded to thirty-eight. Only twenty more were added to the volume issued the year before his death. His last work, *The New Atlantis*, a shrewdly prophetic treatise on political philosophy in the form of a fable, was never finished.

Paul van Somer (1576-1621) shows Bacon in the full tide of worldly success.

> And thou, who didst the stars and sunbeams know,
> Self-school'd, self-scann'd, self-honour'd, self-secure,
> Didst walk on Earth unguessed at.

OF the myriad comments on Shakespeare and his powers which have issued from his day to our own, none is more succinct than Matthew Arnold's sonnet. 'Others abide our question,' as Arnold said: Shakespeare is free.

He was born at Stratford-on-Avon – a town now almost given over to the celebration of his fame – in 1564, during the reign of Elizabeth I. He came to London at the age of about twenty-two, and rarely left the capital until, having made his fortune by and through the theatre, he retired to his native place, where he died on 23 April 1611, a day dedicated to the memory of St George, patron saint of England.

The span of Shakespeare's creative life was, as it seems likely, between 1591, when he produced the three parts of *Henry VI*, and the writing of *The Tempest*, dating from some twenty years later, when Elizabeth had been succeeded by James I. Tragedies, comedies, histories, poems, all yield their abundant riches.

Two portraits are held to be authentic: the bust by Gerald Janssen in Stratford Church, and the frontispiece to the Folio edition of the plays. The First Folio appeared in 1623 and included all completed plays except *Pericles*. The engraving by Martin Droeshout (*fl.* 1620-1651), which adorns successive editions, bears out characteristics of the monument. It gives posterity an idea of Shakespeare's outward appearance, but makes no attempt to probe beneath the surface of the prodigy who wrote, not for a select audience, but for all men for all time.

MANY Elizabethans had short lives: Ben Jonson survived well into the reign of Charles I. He had among his acquaintances William Drummond of Hawthornden (1585-1649) who recorded his conversation, and Inigo Jones (1573-1652) whose designs and dresses, almost as well known as his architecture, embellished some of Jonson's masques, entertainments devised for the pleasure of the Court.

After a precarious early life, in the course of which he killed an actor in a duel, Jonson wrote *Every Man in his Humour*, which was performed in 1598 with Shakespeare in the cast, and in the following year *Every Man out of his Humour*, which was seen at the Globe. His first extant tragedy, *Sejanus*, was performed in 1603: two years later his first masque was staged, the collaboration with Inigo Jones continuing until 1630, when a quarrel led to the loss of Jonson's Court patronage.

Among Jonson's greater plays are three written between 1605 and 1610, *Volpone or the Fox*, *Epicoene or the Silent Woman*, and *The Alchemist*, but he continued to write to the end of his life, and in time he was received back into royal favour. He had always kept the respect of his fellow writers, and this extended to men such as Robert Herrick (1591-1674) and Sir John Suckling (1609-1642), far younger than himself, whom he was pleased to call his 'sons'.

In person Jonson was tall and swarthy, his face marked with smallpox. An unknown artist shows him as he was in later life. He was buried in Westminster Abbey, an admirer causing a mason to cut in the slab over his grave the words: 'O Rare Ben Jonson'.

12

JOHN DONNE

1573-1631

JOHN DONNE, son of a London ironmonger, became secretary to the Keeper of the Great Seal, but temporarily lost favour by his second marriage to Anne More, a niece of his patron's wife. He sailed in two expeditions under the Earl of Essex, an experience reflected in his poems 'The Storm' and 'The Calm'. In 1615, eschewing his earlier Catholicism, he took Anglican orders, and was made Chaplain to James I. He soon established himself as a preacher of unsurpassed range and power. For the last ten years of his life Donne was Dean of St Paul's, and often preached before the young King Charles I. It was his pleasure to erect a monument to himself, dressed in his shroud, executed by Nicholas Stone (1586-1647). It was one of the few which survived the Great Fire of London.

His sermons apart, Donne's fame was posthumous, and even the Sermons were not collected until 1640. In verse he wrote satires, epistles, elegies, love poems. They are distinguished by wit, profundity and complexity of thought, by passion and subtlety, allied with vigorous roughness of form.

'I sing not Syren-like to tempt; for I am harsh.' Thus Donne wrote, and thus it was; but he was the greatest of those 'metaphysical' poets in whose work fire mingles with hard reason. An imperfect collection of his poems was published two years after his death, and another in 1649. It is only within our own time that satisfactory texts have been established, and, as succeeding generations find, few writers yield more treasure.

Donne was painted, the year after his appointment to the royal household, by Isaac Oliver (d. 1617). Oliver ranks among the best of all miniaturists, a form of art in which this country then excelled.

Reproduced by gracious permission of Her Majesty the Queen

13

ROBERT HERRICK

1591-1674

A LONDONER by birth, Herrick was first apprenticed to his uncle, Sir William Herrick, who was a goldsmith. He then went to St John's College, Cambridge, took Holy Orders, and was presented by Charles I to the living of Dean Prior, a remote Devonshire parish. There he lived for nearly twenty years, till he was ejected as the result of the disturbances of the English Civil War.

During the days of the Commonwealth Herrick was again in London, but his parish was restored to him soon after the return of Charles II, and from 1662 until his death twelve years later, he remained a parish priest.

Herrick's more serious poems, of which there are a number, were collected in 1647 under the title of *Noble Numbers or Pious Pieces*, a suitable title for stern times. His better known *Hesperides or Works both Human and Divine*, which included the only portrait known, was issued in the year following, although some sixty of its twelve hundred items had already been published anonymously in a collection called *Wit's Recreation*.

As a lyric poet, Herrick stands high for the sweetness, grace, and occasional poetic fire which infused his work. His 'Anthea', and 'Gather Ye Rosebuds while Ye May', though over-familiar, are unsurpassed in their kind, while his more serious verse such as the 'Litany to the Holy Ghost', less well-known, shows that Herrick had a side to his nature which, though not often called to mind, drew respect from weightier men.

Tempora cinxisset Foliorum densior umbra:
  Debetur Genio laurea Sylva tuo.
Tempora et Illa Tibi mollis redimisset Oliva;
  Scilicet excludis Versibus Arma tuis.
Admisces Antiqua Novis, Iucunda Severis:
  Hinc Iuvenis discat, Fœmina, Virgo, Senex.
Ut solo minor es Phœbo, sic major es Unus
  Omnibus, Ingenio, Mente, Lepore, Stylo.

W. Marshall Fecit.   scripsit I.H.C. W. M.

GEORGE HERBERT, a younger brother of Lord Herbert of Cherbury (1583-1648) philosopher and historian, was educated at Westminster and Trinity College, Cambridge, where he took his degree and later became Public Orator. He was the friend of Donne and Walton, and of a still older writer, Francis Bacon, who held him in much esteem.

In earlier life Herbert attached himself to the Court, in the hope of advancement, but later he came under the influence of Nicholas Ferrar (1592-1637) and of the contemplative community which Ferrar established at Little Gidding in Huntingdonshire. Herbert was ordained deacon in 1626 and was appointed Prebend of Leighton Bromswold, in Ferrar's county, where he rebuilt the church. In 1630 he was ordained priest and became Rector of Bemerton in Wiltshire, where he passed the rest of his brief life, discharging the duties of a parish priest with exemplary scruple.

Herbert wrote some admirable prose, which includes *A Priest to the Temple*, described by Walton as enshrining 'plain, prudent, useful rules for the county parson'. His enduring fame derives from *The Temple, or Sacred Poems and Private Ejaculations*, a collection of verse which was issued soon after his death, and which won wide recognition, among its admirers being Charles I. Almost certainly, an extant Bodleian manuscript was the one which Herbert sent to Ferrar from his death-bed, charging his friend 'if he can think it may turn to the advantage of any dejected poor soul, let it be made publick.' Most properly, Ferrar gave the world this fine expression of Anglican faith. Walton, in his *Life* of 1670, added an engraved portrait based on a drawing by R. White, which is the only representation of Herbert to have survived.

IZAAK WALTON

1593-1683

ANGLER and biographer, the writer of the classic treatise on coarse-fishing and of model lives of John Donne, Sir Henry Wotton (1568-1639), Richard Hooker (?1554-1600), George Herbert and Bishop Sanderson (1587-1663) all but one of whom were his contemporaries, Izaak Walton had a long and enviable life, and the strife in church and State which marked his age seems to have touched him little.

Born at Stafford, he was apprenticed to an ironmonger, and later continued in trade on his own account. His success was such that he was able to enjoy the society of eminent, good and learned men. He also fished his streams, and he spent his later years at Winchester, where his son occupied a prebendary's stall. There he lies buried.

Walton's four earlier *Lives* were first collected in 1670, and the last, that of Sanderson, was written when he was eighty-five. They reflect his goodness, his perceptive charity, and his interest in ecclesiastical matters, a side of his nature reinforced by marriage first to Rachel Floud, a kinswoman of Archbishop Cranmer (1489-1556) and then, after Rachel's death, to Ann, half-sister of Bishop Ken (1637-1711) famous as a hymn-writer.

The *Compleat Angler*, a discourse in dialogue form which is managed with unobtrusive skill, was issued first in 1653 and met with immediate success. There were five editions during Walton's lifetime, and to the fifth, that of 1676, the author's friend Charles Cotton (1630-1687), another Staffordshire man, added a continuation on fly-fishing, about which Walton knew little. Wise in most things, Walton chose a good artist for his portrait, and it is through Jacob Huysmans (?1633-1696) that posterity is enabled to see him.

'Look not for Whales in the Euxine Sea,' wrote Sir Thomas Browne in *Christian Morals*, 'or great matters where they are not to be found.' It is vain to search in *Religio Medici*, *Pseudodoxia Epidemica*, *Urn Burial*, the *Garden of Cyrus* or even the posthumous *Christian Morals* itself for a strictly systematical scheme of thought, but of flowers there are plenty, and Browne's ornate prose, rich in curious learning and stately rhyme, continues to attract.

Browne was the son of a London merchant who after an education at Winchester and Pembroke College, Oxford, studied medicine on the Continent, at Montpellier, Padua and Leyden. Then he settled at Norwich, where he flourished for the rest of his life. A royalist by conviction, he managed to avoid taking part in the Civil War, but was knighted by Charles II in 1671 while the King was on a visit to the East Anglian capital.

Typical of Browne's eloquence was *Urn Burial*, which was published in 1658, together with the *Garden of Cyrus*. Herein the author discussed the various modes of burial which antiquaries believed had been used in Britain. The tone, from the first grave words: 'When the Funerall pyre was out, and the last valediction over' to the closing passage: 'But the iniquity of oblivion blindly scattereth her poppy' is meditative and mystical, sometimes reaching to the highest level of rhetorical expression. Browne was a writer who enjoyed using his powers, and no theme was too recondite to attract him.

Browne married Dorothy Mileham, and in the earliest known portrait, painted before 1650 by Joan Carlile (*fl.* 1640-1650) he is seen with his wife.

JOHN MILTON

No poet has ever been more rightly certain of his own powers than Milton. In prose, he was often gnarled and tendencious. In verse, he rose, like the Spirit in 'Comus' –

> Above the smoak and stir of this dim spot
> Which men call Earth . . .

– into realms of majestic imagination, and with a gift of eloquence and harmony unequalled.

A Londoner born, Milton went to St Paul's School and to Christ's College, Cambridge. At the University he composed some of the best of his earlier poetry. When still a young man, he journeyed in France and Italy, then, thinking it 'base to be travelling for amusement abroad while my fellow citizens are fighting for liberty at home,' he returned to engage in politics and controversy. He was employed as Latin Secretary to the Commonwealth Government after the execution of Charles I, and continued as such, despite increasing blindness, until the Restoration.

Paradise Lost, Milton's epic, was begun in 1663 and published in 1667, earning its author a derisory sum. His last major work, *Samson Agonistes*, appeared in 1671 in the same volume as the sequel to his longest poem, *Paradise Regained*, which celebrates man's redemption. In prose the *Areopagitica* of 1644 is best remembered. It is a passionate plea for the freedom of the press. 'Give me liberty to know,' said Milton, 'to utter, and to argue freely, according to conscience, above all liberties.'

Milton portraiture is meagre. An interesting version, long possessed by the Onslow family, is of the poet in his youth *c.* 1629. The painter is not known.

John Milton

EDWARD HYDE, afterwards Earl of Clarendon and the
grandfather of two queens, a notable benefactor to his
own University, Oxford, to which he was devoted, studied
law under his uncle, who was Chief Justice of the King's
Bench, and then entered Parliament. Taking the royal
side in the Civil War, Clarendon followed the Prince of
Wales, later Charles II, into exile, and became his chief
adviser. His daughter Anne married James, Duke of
York, afterwards James II, and became the mother of
Mary, reigning Consort of William III, and of Queen
Anne.

It was in exile that Clarendon began his monumental
History of the Rebellion and Civil Wars in England, full of
character-drawing and with the priceless advantage of
personal knowledge of all the leading protagonists. Clarendon's later life was clouded. Although he became Lord
Chancellor and returned to England in triumph at the
Restoration, he was never popular, and in 1667 he was
arraigned and disgraced, nominally for the lack of success of the country's foreign policy. Clarendon fled to
France, first to Montpelier and then to Rouen, where he
died.

The *History* did not appear in print until 1702-1704,
and even then in an unsatisfactory edition, though the
profits enabled the Clarendon printing-house in Broad
Street, Oxford, to be established. The autobiography
which Clarendon wrote during his second exile was not
issued until 1759. Able but unlucky, his fame was posthumous. He enriched the annals of his country by pro-
viding a matchless though partial account of the extended
tragedy of the reign of Charles I. Among those who
painted Clarendon was Sir Peter Lely (1618-1680).
Clarendon is shown at the height of his fame, after the
Restoration and before his impeachment.

NOTHING better illustrates that it is possible to be fair to opponents, even in a time of deadly strife, than Marvell's 'Horatian Ode upon Cromwell's return from Ireland'. Composed in 1650, when Marvell was in the household of Lord Fairfax, the Parliamentary General, and loud in its praise of Cromwell, Marvell paid an unforgettable tribute to the martyred Charles I, who 'nothing common did nor mean' at the time of his trial, and who, at the last, when brought to the scaffold:

> Bow'd his comely head
> Down, as upon a bed.

Born near Hull, and educated there and at Trinity College, Cambridge, Marvell shone in everything he did. His poems, 'To His Coy Mistress', 'Thoughts in a Garden', 'The Emigrants in the Bermudas' and a succession of others, are musical and subtle. The satire which he wrote after the Restoration has wit and sting. His defence of Milton, with whom he at one time shared duties as Latin Secretary, and his praise of *Paradise Lost* showed generosity as well as perception; while for many years, as Member of Parliament for his native city, he wrote letters to his constituents on public matters which were shrewd and conscientious, and are of permanent value to the historian.

Marvell's poems were not collected until 1681, after his death, and even then the satires were not included. His portrait was painted, almost certainly before the Restoration, by an artist who may have been John Hayls (*d.* 1679) who painted Samuel Pepys, though this attribution is tentative. John Aubrey (1626-1697) who knew and valued Marvell, described him as 'of a middling stature, pretty strong sett, roundish faced, cherry-cheek't, hazell eie, browne hair.'

JOHN BUNYAN, author of *The Pilgrim's Progress*, was
born at Elstow, near Bedford, the son of a tin-smith or
tinker. Set to learn his father's trade, he was soon caught
up in the strife between Charles I and his Parliament.
For some two years Bunyan served in the Parliamentary
army. During the time of the Commonwealth he joined
a Nonconformist church at Bedford, and after the restoration of the monarchy he was arrested for preaching
without a licence.

Bunyan was in prison for twelve years, during which
time he supported his wife and a family of four children,
including a blind girl, by making tagged laces and by
writing books, the most important among them being
Grace Abounding to the Chief of Sinners (1666), a narrative
which includes details of his own religious and secular
experiences. Released in 1672, Bunyan continued writing and preaching, but he began his most famous work
during a second term of imprisonment, publishing it in
1678. The early editions were read to pieces: so popular
were they, that surviving copies are of the highest rarity.
Bunyan's sturdy prose, informed with burning conviction, carries the reader headlong into successive adventures, always identifying himself with the pilgrim and his
cause, just as the author intended.

Bunyan died in 1688, and was buried in Bunhill Fields
in the City of London. Robert White (1645-1703) drew
him from life.

POET, dramatist, satirist, critic and translator, Dryden was born at Aldwinkle All Saints in Northamptonshire, of a family inclined to the Puritan side in religion and politics. His first considerable poem eulogised Oliver Cromwell, but the Restoration brought tribute in 'Astraea Redux', and Dryden was soon in demand as a dramatist, the most lasting of his plays being *All for Love*, which was based on Shakespeare's *Antony and Cleopatra*, and *Marriage-à-la Mode*.

Dryden found his richest vein in satire. He gave and took hard knocks, and in 1681 he wrote, in *Absalom and Achitophel*, one of the best sustained poems of its kind in any language. In later life he joined the Church of Rome, and he was deprived of the Poet Laureateship, which he had held for nearly twenty years when, in 1688, the advent of William of Orange ensured a Protestant succession. In his own view, some of his best poetry belonged to his later years, for instance the second of two poems in honour of St Cecilia's day, 'Alexander's Feast', which he wrote for a musical society in 1697. His 'Ode on the Death of Mr Henry Purcell' (1696) commemorates his association with a great composer.

Although Dryden is best remembered as a poet, his prose and his criticism, in particular his *Essay of Dramatic Poesy*, which opens to the sound of Dutch gun-fire in the Thames, are almost as memorable. Sir Godfrey Kneller (1646-1723), the fashionable portrait painter of his time, made several versions of Dryden in his splendour.

PEPYS's place in a gallery given to men of letters is by virtue of the most honest and entertaining diary in the language. He was the son of a London tailor, and he had a good education at St Paul's and at Cambridge. He married young, and entered the household of Edward Montagu, later Earl of Sandwich. His patron's help enabled him to embark on an official career, in which he rose in due time to become Secretary of the Admiralty. His later fortune was checkered, but until his final withdrawal into private life he strove, whenever he was in office, to ensure that the country had an efficient Fleet.

Pepys met everyone of consequence, from Charles II downwards, and his diary, which opens on 1 January 1660, continues until 31 May 1669, the year in which his wife died. He also wrote an account of a visit to Tangiers, made in 1683. The diary remained in Thomas Skelton's system of shorthand at Magdalene College, Cambridge, until 1825, when it was transcribed by John Smith and edited by Lord Braybrooke. It was realised that a record of the highest interest had come to light. Its popularity ever since has never been in doubt.

The diarist was musical, and a keen student of plays and literature of his time. One of those who painted him, John Hayls (*d.* 1679), shows Pepys in an Indian gown with a scroll on which is a song he wrote – 'Beauty retire'. An entry for 11 April 1666 records that the musical touch 'pleases me mightily, it being painted true.'

DANIEL DEFOE

?1661-1731

IF to delight the young, for generation after generation, is a proof of vitality, the author of *Robinson Crusoe*, the prototype of the desert-island story, had it in full measure. Defoe's industry was incessant, his life largely underground. The son of a London butcher called Foe, Daniel, who was a Dissenter, fought as a young man in Monmouth's rebellion, and was lucky to escape punishment. In 1688 he joined the party of William of Orange, and for the rest of his long life he was engaged in political activity of one kind or another, often in trouble, occasionally in prison or at the pillory, at other times working in government interest. About the year 1703, he added a De to his surname.

Over the years, a flood of prose poured out: controversy, commentary, travel, history, journalism and a series of novels written with detailed verisimilitude and an unfailing flow of narrative invention. *Captain Singleton*, *Moll Flanders*, *Journal of the Plague Year*, the *Memoirs of a Cavalier*, the perennial *Robinson Crusoe*, which first appeared in 1719, these are well known, but Defoe's full bibliography is long, complex, fascinating in variety, for his energy and skill were prodigious. He travelled, engaged in merchandising and knew as much as any man of the broad events of world politics and the ramifications of international trade.

No portrait of Defoe is known, beyond the frontispiece engraved by Michael van der Gucht (1660-1725) for the author's *Jure Divino* of 1707.

M. V. Gucht Sculp.

SWIFT, after an Irish upbringing, was admitted to the household of Sir William Temple (1628-1699), diplomat, writer and patron. In 1694 he was ordained, then, returning under Temple's roof, he began his literary career in 1704 with the publication of *The Battle of the Books* and *A Tale of a Tub*, which satirised 'corruption in literature and learning' with an effect which startled every reader.

For the rest of his life, Swift engaged in incessant polemics, generally in opposition. In 1713 he was made Dean of St Patrick's, his only advancement, and his hatred and contempt for mankind increased as age, disappointment and increasing disease, which in the end involved madness, clouded his majestic, bitter mind. In 1726 he published *Gulliver's Travels*, his most lastingly popular work, the adventures which are unfolded having survived its immediate satirical purpose. Swift was the great master of irony, depicting the ideal and pretending to believe in its reality – humorously noting the real, and affecting to believe it ideal.

Swift had love affairs with Esther (Stella) Johnson, Temple's natural daughter, the object of his *Journal to Stella*, and with Esther van Homrigh, the Vanessa of his correspondence. The rupture of their friendship led to Vanessa's death, while that of Stella, in 1728, deprived Swift of the one person he really loved, and may secretly have married.

Swift was painted by Charles Jervas (?1675-1739).

BORN in Yorkshire, but taken as a child to Ireland, where his father was serving in the army, Congreve was at Kilkenny School and at Trinity College, Dublin, being a fellow pupil with Swift. Returning to England, he attended the Middle Temple as a law student, but his immediate future was decided by the success of his comedy, *The Old Batchelor*, to which the acting of Anne Bracegirdle (1663-1748) much contributed. Anne and Congreve were thenceforth associated, and Congreve went from strength to strength with *The Double Dealer*, *Love for Love* and *The Mourning Bride*, his only tragedy. Congreve, Wycherley and the outlook which their plays reflected was attacked in 1698 by Jeremy Collier (1650-1726) in *A Short View of the Immorality and Profaneness of the English Stage*. This return to Puritanism actually led to Congreve's prosecution, and to the fining of Anne Bracegirdle and others. It was because of the change of climate that the supreme work of its kind, Congreve's *The Way of the World* (1700), which so pleases modern audiences, was ill received, an event which decided the author to abandon further writing for the stage.

By the time he gave up literary work, Congreve was in prosperous circumstances, and was highly regarded by his intellectual peers. He retained his friendship with Swift; he was on familiar terms with Steele and Pope; and he was visited by Voltaire (1694-1778). In later life his sight failed him.

Sir Godfrey Kneller (1646-1723) painted Congreve as a member of the Kit-Cat Club, named after the kit-cats or mutton pies which were a feature of its gatherings.

JOSEPH ADDISON

1672-1719

EDUCATED at Charterhouse and at the Queen's College, Oxford, Addison, son of the Dean of Lichfield, travelled on the Continent, at Government expense, in preparation for a life of diplomacy, and at the age of thirty-four was made Under-Secretary of State. His career, during the course of which he held a succession of public appointments, was crowned by his acceptance of a Commissionship for Trade. His marriage in 1716 to the Dowager Countess of Warwick added little to his happiness.

Addison wrote hymns and secular verse, and was a popular member of the Kit-cat Club, but his best contribution to letters arose from the outlook of a scholar and traveller, the good sense, charm and moderation which he brought to journalism, especially by contributions he made to the *Tatler*, which was started by Sir Richard Steele (1672-1729) in 1709. Addison and Steele both had a hand in the creation of Sir Roger de Coverley, an old-fashioned Worcester baronet of memorable parts. The two men were also associated with the *Spectator*, which became the *Tatler's* successor, its object being 'to enliven morality with wit, and to transform wit with morality.' Addison and Steele were estranged towards the end of Addison's life, but they set their mark upon eighteenth-century prose, helping to raise the standard of manners and elegance in life and letters.

Addison figures in the collection of Kit-Cat portraits by Sir Godfrey Kneller (1646-1723).

THE son of a Catholic linen-draper with a business in London, Pope's health was undermined and his figure distorted by the age of twelve through what was put down to 'perpetual application'. Brought up at Binfield in Windsor Forest, he was largely self-educated, showing at a very early age the metrical skill upon which part of his fame rests.

William Wycherley (1640-1716), the dramatist, introduced Pope to London life, and his *Essay on Criticism*, written in heroic couplets, published at first anonymously, brought the author credit and began to make him respected. Comparative affluence came with a version of Homer's *Iliad*, which made £5,000. This was succeeded by a rendering of the *Odyssey*, equally acceptable to the taste of the day. Pope was no professional scholar, and his assistants William Browne (1689-1745) and Elijah Fenton (1683-1730) caught his style so closely as almost to defy identification.

Pope bought a villa at Twickenham where he lived and flourished, courted by many and feared by more for his caustic tongue and pen. He could be a staunch friend, and he was a devoted son, but he did not spare those whom he considered enemies or fools. His *Dunciad* is eloquent venom, and he was capable of protracted malice. Pope's tireless industry was mainly engaged upon what he did well, and there were spheres in which he excelled. 'The Rape of the Lock', for instance, is the best mock-heroic poem in the language, and the 'Essay on Man' has unforgettable passages.

Like Swift, Pope was painted by Charles Jervas (?1675-1739). The artist shows him with Martha Blount (1690-1762) to whom he was attached.

SAMUEL RICHARDSON, whose father was a joiner of Derby, was a successful printer who turned novelist late in life, the result of circumstance rather than inner compulsion. He prospered in his London business to such a degree that he undertook the Journals of the House of Commons; then, in 1740, at the request of two of his fellow-craftsmen, he prepared 'a little volume of letters, in a common style, on such subjects as might be of use to country readers who are unable to indite for themselves.' This was the germ of *Pamela*, which developed into a story which struck a genuine if over-protracted note of sentiment. It had a maid-servant instead of a fashionable woman as heroine, and it went straight to the heart of the common reader.

Pamela was followed by *Clarissa Harlowe*, which is generally accounted Richardson's masterpiece, and surpassed even its precursor in popularity, bringing the author European fame – this despite a sad fate for its heroine, and death in a duel for the man who abducted her. Richardson composed a final novel, *Sir Charles Grandison*, which appeared in 1754, with a happy ending. It expressed his ideal of a Christian gentleman. The theme of all three works – that only through means of a wedding ring should a man be admitted to a woman's bed-chamber – admits of infinite reversals and stratagems to illuminate the sex-war which was Richardson's subject.

Described as a 'stout, rosy, vain, prosy little man', this is the character caught, though with affection, by Joseph Highmore (1692-1780), who illustrated the novels to their author's satisfaction.

S: Richardson
Author of Clarissa.

HAVING burlesqued contemporary playwrights in *Tom Thumb*, and laughed at Richardson in his first novel, *Joseph Andrews*, which included Pamela's brother Joseph in the character of a footman, Fielding was soon challenged by the seriousness and problems of the novelist's craft. He proceeded to write, in *Tom Jones*, what many consider the greatest novel in the language.

The author's insight, wide knowledge of life, humanity and wisdom were based upon broad experience, particularly in the law, which he had studied at Leyden and the Middle Temple and practised on the Western Circuit, and in political journalism. He became a magistrate of exemplary diligence, like his blind half-brother, and a satirist of power, as was shown in *The History of Jonathan Wild the Great*, which exposed what the world was pleased to call 'greatness' in vigorous fashion. Fielding's final novel, *Amelia*, was intended to illustrate some of the evils which he had met with in the course of his duties, particularly those of the sponging-houses and prisons.

Fielding wore himself out. In 1753, seriously ill, he went to Lisbon by sea with a somewhat slender hope of recovery, and died in the Portuguese capital, his last work being a Journal of the voyage. There is no satisfactory portrait, but William Hogarth (1697-1764) made a sketch of the author for an edition issued in 1762. Seeing it, Hazlitt remarked that Fielding had 'that interested physiognomy that binds and concentrates.'

HENRY FIELDING, Ætatis XLVIII.

JOHNSON'S is the triumph of life over letters, for although he left behind him a Dictionary, a few excellent poems, many essays, a short novel, *Rasselas*, a dull tragedy, *Irene*, critical notes on Shakespeare, and lives of poets, it is not so much for these he is remembered as because Boswell, his biographer, made him such an engrossing character that he casts his shadow upon an age. Posterity knows no man better, and surely no man was better worth knowing.

He was the son of a Lichfield bookseller, educated in his native town and at Pembroke College, Oxford. For a time he kept a school, then he rode to London, with a wife much older than himself, hoping to make his fortune by writing. It was a long struggle. Johnson was learned, lazy, devout, charitable and fearless. He had nothing of the sycophant, and his sympathy went where it was deserved, not where it paid. The tide turned in 1755 with the publication of the *Dictionary*, the most readable ever printed. For nearly thirty years, though never affluent, he was increasingly respected for the breadth of his interests, his powers of perception, his conversation, and not least for his goodness. There was, as Goldsmith said, 'nothing of the bear but his skin.'

Johnson's critical blindness was sometimes as apparent as his shortness of physical sight, but his wrong-headedness is never pedantry. Joseph Nollekens (1737-1823), who, as Johnson said, could chop a head as well as anyone, created a monument for him in Westminster Abbey.

STERNE had a genius for turning things upside down. Born in Ireland, he went to Jesus College, Cambridge. Later he lived at Sutton-in-the-Forest, Yorkshire, where he held a cure of souls, to which was added, through the influence of his wife, a prebendary's stall. In 1760 the first two volumes of his highly original novel *Tristram Shandy* were published, and Sterne hastened to London to see how they were received. There was no doubt of their welcome, and others soon followed – volume three containing the preface! Soon there were a host of followers of Walter Shandy, my uncle Toby, Corporal Trim, Yorick the parson, Dr Slop, and the widow Wadman. Sterne had invented a new sort of story, which made nonsense of time.

Tristram Shandy was completed by 1767. Sterne had meanwhile published the *Sermons of Mr Yorick* and in 1768 he followed up his novel with *A Sentimental Journey through France and Italy* in much the same inconsequential style. The book was to have consisted of four volumes, but only two were finished. The author's behaviour grew as extravagant as his books. He neglected his family, ruined his health, and died insolvent in lodgings in Old Bond Street, his corpse being followed to the grave by a coach containing his publisher and one other mourner. There was a final adventure. Sterne's body was exhumed, and it appeared shortly afterwards upon the table of the professor of Anatomy at his old University.

The best-known study of Sterne, by an unknown artist, shows him in the canonicals he wore so lightly.

GRAY was a Londoner, the son of a scrivener, and was sent to Eton and to Peterhouse, Cambridge, from which he later migrated across the street to Pembroke College as the result of a practical joke which played upon his fear of fire. At Eton he had met Horace Walpole, with whom he travelled in France and Italy. When he returned home, it was to settle in Cambridge for the rest of his life. Gray and Walpole quarrelled, but they were later reconciled, and it was Walpole's pleasure to publish some of Gray's best verse.

Although his output was neither regular nor considerable, Gray was offered the Poet Laureateship on the strength of his 'Ode on a Distant Prospect of Eton College' and a series of Pindaric odes. He declined; but in 1768 he accepted the Cambridge Professorship of Modern History, which suited his tastes and entailed only nominal duties.

Gray published his 'Elegy in a Country Churchyard', which is generally identified with Stoke Poges, in 1751. Its composition had been begun as early as 1742, and its perfection was the result of infinite care. Samuel Johnson, who did not much care for Gray, spoke bare truth when he said that the *Elegy* 'abounds with images which find a mirror in every mind, and with sentiments to which every heart returns an echo.'

Apart from his poetry, Gray wrote a Journal of travel among the English Lakes which was published soon after his death, and his letters were among the best of their time. Like Horace Walpole, Gray was painted by John Giles Eccardt (*c.* 1740-1779).

HORACE WALPOLE was the fourth son of Sir Robert Walpole (1676-1745), who long held office as the Prime Minister of George II. Horace was educated at Eton and King's College, Cambridge, and after travel with Gray, he settled, like Pope, at Twickenham, where he turned Strawberry Hill, his villa, into 'a little Gothic castle'. He established a printing press, useful for his own productions as well as for the poems of his friends. His *Anecdotes of Painting in England* and the *Catalogue of Engravers* which followed it, remain valuable to art historians.

Walpole's 'Gothic Story', *The Castle of Otranto*, appeared in 1764, full of melodrama, ghosts and horrors, and was the prototype of many less successful ventures. His reputation rests mainly upon his letters, which make an engrossing series, his correspondents including Sir Horace Mann, who for nearly half a century was British envoy at Florence, Field Marshal Conway, who was Walpole's cousin, the Countess of Upper Ossory, and many others. His letters to Madame du Deffand (1697-1780) were destroyed by his own wish, though hers to him have survived. Walpole knew everyone, saw everything, noted every scrap of gossip. He was in Parliament from 1741 to 1767 but took no great part in public business. In his old age he succeeded to the earldom of Orford.

Eccardt's portrait of 1754 shows a kindly, contemplative man about whom, thanks to his own historical sense, it is possible to know much, and whose industry was mainly employed with the good sense which matched his remarkable taste.

BORN in Dumbartonshire, Smollett went to the University of Glasgow, then, having picked up some knowledge of medicine, and seeking livelihood and adventure, he sailed as a surgeon's mate on board H.M.S. *Chichester*, in which he was present at an abortive attack on Cartagena during war with Spain. Naval life on the West Indian station horrified but fascinated him, and when he returned home and discovered gifts as a novelist in the picaresque tradition, he was able to draw an arresting series of characters from the sea profession. *Roderick Random*, with its account of Cartagena, is largely autobiographical, and is calculated to give the reader a thorough distaste for the Navy. *Peregrine Pickle*, which followed it, included Commodore Hawser Trunnion, the ferocity of whose language is equalled only be the kindness of his heart. In *Humphry Clinker* Smollett was land-bound: many believe it to be his best work.

Novels were only one side, though the most lasting, of Smollett's activity. He translated *Don Quixote*. He edited a journal, *The Critical Review*, and later *The Briton*, political in tinge. He wrote an extensive *History of England*, and he even attempted a farce, *The Reprisal*. Ill health sent him abroad in 1763, and three years later he published the entertaining though ill-tempered *Travels in France and Italy* which brought him (from Sterne of all people) the nick-name of Smellfungus.

The principal portrait is by the hand of an artist unknown, but a pawky character emerges, very much alive.

WHEN Samuel Johnson was wandering about London in search of fortune, he made acquaintance with a younger writer, William Collins. He was later able to include Collins among the poets whose lives he wrote, recalling him as a man 'with whom I once delighted to converse, and whom I yet remember with tenderness.'

Collins, who in his *Odes* wrote some of the best examples of their difficult kind, was born at Chichester, his father being a hatter. Educated at Winchester and Magdalen College, Oxford, he drifted to London, hoping to win fame with his verse. Some of it is lost: what remains is precious, particularly the 'Ode to Evening', which in feeling if not in language anticipates the Romantics; the 'Ode to Simplicity', and the 'Ode written in the Beginning of the Year 1746' during the War of the Austrian Succession. Collins was a friend of James Thomson (1700-1748) author of *The Seasons*, whose death he commemorated. Unlike Johnson's, his generous biographer, Collins's own fortunes never mended, and this may partly have been his own fault. Johnson records that he once rescued Collins from trouble at the hands of the bailiffs by obtaining the promise of a bookseller to publish a new version of Aristotle's *Poetics*. Collins took the guineas, repaid them soon afterwards as the result of a legacy, but never finished the translation. His poems continued to be little regarded in his life-time and he died, deranged, at his sister's house at Chichester.

A portrait by Bellars, made when the poet was a boy, was engraved for an edition published in 1804.

CHRISTOPHER SMART was another poor poet whom Johnson befriended, proof enough, if any were needed, of the breath of his sympathy, for he was of an utterly different kind from the successes of his own day, a man whose work was valued by the Romantics, and still later judges, more than by contemporaries. He was born at Shipbourne in Kent, and was sent by the help of the Duchess of Cleveland to Pembroke College, Cambridge, where there is an admirable though unsigned portrait, showing a rotund and rather dandified figure, proud of a commendation from Pope which is clearly shown. Later, in London, Smart tried to live by writing, but he fell into debt, and was confined in a madhouse, whence issued his splendid *Song to David*, original, powerful, lyrical, in honour of the Psalmist.

Boswell recorded the following conversation, which took place in the year 1763. 'How does poor Smart do, sir?' enquired Johnson's friend Dr Burney: 'is he likely to recover?' *Johnson:* 'It seems as if his mind had ceased to struggle with the disease: for he grows fat upon it.' *Burney:* 'Perhaps, sir, that may be for want of exercise.' *Johnson:* 'No, sir, he has partly as much exercise as he used to have, for he digs in his garden. Indeed, before his confinement, he used for exercise to walk to the ale-house; but he was *carried* back again. I did not think he ought to be shut up. His infirmities were not noxious to society. He insisted on people praying with him; and I'd as lief pray with Kit Smart as any one else. Another charge was, that he did not love clean linen: and I have no passion for it.'

'THE oak of the forest did not grow there,' wrote Boswell of Goldsmith, 'but the elegant shrubbery and the fragrant parterre appeared in gay succession.' Oliver Goldsmith was Irish. Born in 1730 and educated at Trinity College, Dublin, he wandered about Europe before arriving in London in 1756, destitute. He had acquired some knowledge of medicine on his travels, but practised with small success. A turn of fortune came with the sale of a short novel, *The Vicar of Wakefield*, to a bookseller, for £60. Samuel Johnson made the bargain, and so it proved, for it is always in print, always admired for its kindly delineation of the Primrose family and their adventures.

Goldsmith wrote copiously for bread, and spent or gave away what he earned without thought for the future. Besides his novel, he wrote poems which include 'The Traveller' and 'The Deserted Village', and plays, one of which, *She Stoops to Conquer*, was first produced at Covent Garden in 1773 and has been enjoyed ever since.

Goldsmith died the year after his stage success, and was buried in the Temple Church. There is a monument to him in Westminster Abbey, put up by Johnson's famous Literary Club. One of its members, Sir Joshua Reynolds (1723-1792), painted Goldsmith in a version widely known. When he heard news of his death, Reynolds laid down his brush and painted no more that day. Like everyone who knew him, he loved Goldsmith, who possessed, so men said, 'the kindest heart in the world', and who had something else, the power to amuse.

GENERALLY it is necessary to listen to an orator to measure the quality and effect of his powers, for speeches do
not always read well, and in cold print lose much of their
bloom. With Burke it is otherwise. No disquisitions ever
delivered before the House of Commons can be read
today with more profit, more pleasure in the rhythm of
their prose and the richness and variety of their content.

Burke was the second son of an Irish attorney, and he
attended Trinity College, Dublin, later reading law at
the Middle Temple. At the age of twenty-seven he published a treatise *On the Sublime and Beautiful*, full of fresh
ideas and lively speculation. Later he became a friend of
Lord Rockingham (1730-1782), Prime Minister to George
III, entered Parliament, and engaged in the hurly-burly
of political strife, his speeches on Taxation and on Con-
ciliation with the Colonies being among the noblest ex-
pressions brought forth by the War of American Inde-
pendence. In 1782 Burke became Paymaster of the
Forces and a Privy Councillor, and he led the impeachment of Warren Hastings (1733-1818) for corruption and
cruelty in the service of the East India Company, charges
upon which Hastings was eventually acquitted. In later
life Burke's *Reflections on the French Revolution* expressed his
horror at the means by which the ancient government in
France had been overthrown, while a final gesture was
his support for William Wilberforce (1759-1833) in the
earlier stages of his fight to abolish the slave trade. Burke
was a man whose intellectual resources matched the importance of the principles he championed. The best
known portrait came from the studio of Sir Joshua Reynolds (1723-1792).

COWPER's father was rector of Great Berkhampsted, and he sent his son to Westminster. The boy was then articled to a solicitor, and in 1752 had chambers in the Middle Temple. Law was not much to his taste, but when he was offered the comparative haven of a Clerkship at the House of Lords, he was overcome with dread at having to make a formal appearance in the Chamber. The remainder of his life was private. His means were slender, but his capacity for enjoyment of everyday things was wonderful. Had he not had to endure a long struggle against insanity, he could have had an enviably happy life.

Cowper first settled at Huntingdon, and later at Olney in Bedfordshire, where he came under the influence of John Newton (1725-1807), evangelical and hymn-writer. Cowper himself composed hymns, including 'Hark my soul, it is the Lord', which are of lasting appeal; he also wrote much secular verse, including 'The Task', which praised the joys of country life, and at least one humorous favourite, 'John Gilpin'. Among his most effective lines were those on the loss of H.M.S. *Royal George* in 1782 at Spithead: 'Toll for the Brave'.

Cowper loved animals: his tame hares 'Tiny' and 'Puss' and his spaniel 'Beau' were his familiars, and made appearances in his work. His letters, easy and unstudied, give lasting pleasure, and Cowper had no lack of sympathy for those humanitarian issues which engaged the energies of those more active than himself.

Cowper was painted in 1792 by Lemuel Francis Abbott (1760-1803), and the artist found a congenial subject.

To the historian, no writer in the English language stands quite on Gibbon's level. Formally educated at Westminster and Magdalen College, Oxford, Gibbon went abroad when still in his teens, and there he learnt to think. His first work: *Essai sur l'étude de la littérature*, was written in French, and only later translated.

Returning home in 1758, during the course of the Seven Years War, Gibbon served for a time in the Hampshire Militia. Six years later, during a tour in Italy, while 'musing amid the ruins of the Capitol', he formed the plan of his *History of the Decline and Fall of the Roman Empire*, the first volume of which appeared in 1776. The work was eventually completed at Lausanne, the last three volumes of six appearing in 1788.

Gibbon at one time sat in Parliament, but without adding to his reputation. He died in London, his friend Lord Sheffield putting together the *Memoirs* which appeared two years after their author's death.

Less impressive as a man than as a writer, Gibbon, although a member of the Literary Club, would not, as he once murmured, trust himself with Dr Johnson. On paper, he was majestic. His prose, with its incessant antithesis, is as memorable as the sweep of his thought and the learning which reduced a daunting subject into disciplined order. His *Memoirs* add to the impression of a dedicated artist who, though confessedly an indifferent lover, was a faithful friend.

Henry Walton (1746-1813) could not make the dumpy Gibbon into an heroic figure, but his portrait has charm and grace.

BOSWELL revealed Johnson; and by a trick of fate, the discovery of a huge mass of lost material upon which scholars are working, Boswell is himself in the process of being enlarged. Although the revelations are not wholly edifying, who would have expected them to be so?

The biographer was the son of a Scots judge who took the title of Lord Auchinleck from a family property in Ayrshire. He was schooled at Edinburgh, and later studied law in Glasgow and Utrecht, his long-term ambitions being literary.

Boswell had a way of attaching himself to greater men than himself, and one of the subjects of his admiration was General Paoli (1725-1807). He met the Corsican patriot on his travels abroad. Boswell first encountered Johnson in 1763, but their friendship took time to develop and it was a tour which the pair made together in Scotland ten years later, resulting in a Journal from both, that made it certain that if ever Boswell essayed a full scale life, it would be of lasting value. Johnson was no sooner dead than Edmond Malone (1741-1812), a Shakespearian scholar who was by way of being Boswell's literary godfather, applied the necessary pressure to a man of easy-going habits, and the masterpiece appeared in 1791.

Boswell did not neglect the law, and for some two years was Recorder of Carlisle. He survived to enjoy his celebrity, and no one could have savoured it more. His fellow countryman, George Willison (1741-1797) painted Boswell in early life, dandified clothes being in striking contrast with a homely face.

SHERIDAN was born in Dublin, his father being an actor, and he was later at school at Harrow. When aged twenty-one he ran away to France with Elizabeth Ann Linley (1754-1792), a well-known singer, fought two duels with her persecutor, Major Matthews, and married her in 1773.

The young man's career as a dramatist began with *The Rivals* in 1775, continued with the *School for Scandal, St Patrick's Day, The Duenna* and *The Critic*. It ended with a patriotic melodrama, *Pizarro*, adapted from the Spanish. *The Critic* retains interest for its satire on the sentimental drama of its day, and for its depiction of Puff, an advertiser of literary wares who has made a science of his profession. *The Rivals* and *The School for Scandal* keep their appeal on the stage, giving admirable scope for actors and actresses cast for Captain Absolute, Sir Lucius O'Trigger, Lydia Languish and Mrs Malaprop in the first, and the brothers Surface and Lady Teazle in the second. They are examples of the comedy of manners at its brightest.

The dramatist acquired Garrick's share in Drury Lane Theatre in 1776, which he rebuilt in 1791, but he had little head for business and when, in 1809, the theatre was burnt down, he suffered financial distress, and at one time was under arrest for debt.

An admired orator, Sheridan made a name in Parliament, and held posts as Under Secretary for Foreign Affairs, Secretary to the Treasury, and Treasurer of the Navy. In 1788 he was portrayed by John Russell (1745-1806).

FRANCES BURNEY, who later became Madame d'Arblay, was a member of a remarkable family. Her father, Charles Burney (1726-1814) was a musical scholar of high reputation. One of her brothers, James (1750-1821) went round the world with Cook, and became an admiral; another, Charles (1757-1817) was a classical scholar, and yet another, Edward Francis (1760-1840) painted her. Her half-sister Sarah Harriet (?1770-1844) was a fellow novelist. Celebrity came to Frances through *Evelina*, a story which appeared in 1778 at first anonymously, and was praised by Johnson, though he once remarked that he had not read it through.

In 1786 the authoress was offered, and accepted, though with some misgiving, the post of second keeper of the Robes at the Court of Queen Charlotte, wife of George III. Her account of the tedium, jealousies and occasional melodrama of Court life, published many years later in her diary and correspondence, show that she had been right to hesitate, for her health became almost shattered, and she was forced to ask permission to retire.

In 1793 Frances married General D'Arblay, a French officer who had taken refuge in England at the Revolution. She returned with him to his native country during the Peace of Amiens, but was interned by Napoleon. Her later novels, *Cecilia*, *Camilla* and *The Wanderer*, sustained the author's contemporary reputation, though posterity finds more interest in her *Early Diary* (1768-1778) with its sketches of Johnson, Garrick and her father.

CRABBE was born in Suffolk, where his father was a collector of salt dues in the town of Aldeburgh. The boy was apprenticed to a surgeon, but, having little liking for the work, went to London to try his luck as a writer. Burke befriended him, introduced him to Reynolds and others, and encouraged him to publish his poem, 'The Library', which was in the manner of Pope. Next he took orders, becoming chaplain to the Duke of Rutland and preparing, at Belvoir Castle, 'The Village', a poem in heroic couplets which was revised by Burke and Johnson. This made his name as one who knew, and could faithfully describe, the rustic poor.

A long silence followed, until in 1807 Crabbe issued a volume containing 'The Parish Register', which showed marked gifts in narrative. Three years later came 'The Borough', a poem in twenty-four 'letters' which describe life in a country town: it was followed by 'Tales', twenty-one stories in which the poet again showed powers of perception, realism, sometimes humour. In 1814 Crabbe was made Vicar of Trowbridge in Wiltshire, where he spent the rest of his life and where he prepared his final work, 'Tales of the Hall', for which Murray paid £3,000, the sum including unexpired copyrights. Manuscripts found at Crabbe's death and published two years later included at least some work almost equal to what had gone before.

Byron said of Crabbe that he was 'Nature's sternest painter, yet the best'. His outlook was sombre, and it is a melancholy cast of countenance that is caught from the life by H. W. Pickersgill (1782-1875). Crabbe had no illusions about the state of the majority of those with whom he had been brought up.

BLAKE was as much a painter as a writer, and more of a visionary than any artist of his time. The son of a London hosier, he was apprenticed when young to James Basire (1730-1802), engraver to the Society of Antiquaries. Ever afterwards, his aim was to blend his writing with his drawing and painting, the one enhancing the other.

Blake's earliest published work is contained in *Poetical Sketches* which appeared in 1783 partly at the expense of John Flaxman (1755-1826), sculptor and draughtsman. Six years later *Songs of Innocence* revealed Blake's mystical cast of mind more fully, his underlying theme being the all-pervading presence of divine love and sympathy, even in times of sorrow and distress. His principal prose work, *The Marriage of Heaven and Hell* denied the reality of matter, denied eternal punishment, and denied authority.

The *Songs of Experience*, dating from 1794, include several splendid lyrics, while in the Prophetic Books, a whole series of which engaged Blake's powers, he created a mythological world which he illustrated in various media, some of them experimental. He also lavished time and skill on illustrations to appropriate classics, notably to Dante and the Book of Job. Many of Blake's books were bound by his devoted wife, a woman who was as indifferent to worldly values as he was himself.

Blake attracted a few remarkable disciples, among whom was Samuel Palmer (1805-1881), an outstandingly gifted artist, and John Linnell (1792-1882). Linnell did much for Blake's ultimate fame, and in a water-colour portrait of the prophet, he conveyed the gentler side of his nature.

Portrait of
W. BLAKE

J. Linnell Sen'. f.t. 161

The Simile of a Portrait in Ivory
painted from Life by John Linnell 1821

BURNS's poems are close to the heart of every Scot, for a good reason. They express, with a flavour and strength elsewhere unmatched, the sentiments and reflections of the common man.

He was born at Alloway in Ayrshire, and was taught by his father. Put to work as a farm labourer, he soon set up with his brother Gilbert at Mossgiel in his native country, where he wrote 'The Cotter's Saturday Night', 'The Jolly Beggars' and other poems, songs and satires. In 1786 publication of his early work brought him fame, and he was made much of in Edinburgh society. Success also brought him enough money to enable him to marry and to settle at Ellisland in Dumfriesshire, this time on his own farm. He was also given a place as an excise-man which, on the failure of his affairs from literary preoccupation and conviviality, became his principal means of support. The later part of his life was mainly devoted to the composition of a splendid range of songs which include 'Auld Lang Syne', 'My Love is like a red, red rose', and 'Scots wha hae . . .'.

Burns, like most liberal-minded men, had at first sympathised with the French Revolution, but time and the horrors of Paris wrought a change. His last ballad 'Does haughty Gaul invasion threat?' showed the patriotic spirit which led him to join the Dumfriesshire Volunteers. His service was short, for his health failed, and he died when still well short of forty.

Many Scots artists painted their national poet. None captured his appearance and spirit better than Alexander Nasmyth (1758-1840), his contemporary and friend.

DOUGHTY, principled, arrogant and courageous, William Cobbett appeared to sympathisers in his own day like the incarnation of John Bull, and to opponents as something much nearer the Devil. He continues to be read because he wrote vigorous prose, and because he described the light and shade of a countryside which has changed almost beyond recognition.

Cobbett was born at Farnham in Surrey in 1763, the son of a farm labourer. Self-taught, he served in the army, where he rose to the rank of sergeant-major; he travelled and wrote in America; and in 1800 he returned home to become a political journalist. He edited the *Political Register* from 1802 until his death, first with Tory inclinations, then with increasingly radical trends.

Five years before his death in 1835 Cobbett's *Rural Rides* were issued in collected form, and they remain his best memorial. Written as the result of seeing for himself the effects of the acute agricultural depression which followed the protracted war against Revolutionary and Napoleonic France, Cobbett suggested his remedies, and trounced opponents in the process. His career as a journalist and in Parliament is largely forgotten, but the figure of Cobbett astride his mount ranging through a lovely though then melancholy countryside will remain vivid as long as readers enjoy fresh description fired with the enthusiasm to improve.

Cobbett looked much like what he was, and Adam Buck (1759-1833) who drew him from the life in 1819, caught the essence of a formidable, practical, original man.

WORDSWORTH, the longest lived of those who gave impetus to the movement styled Romantic, away from what was considered to be the artificiality of Pope and his successors, was born at Cockermouth in Cumberland, the son of an attorney. He went to school at Hawkshead and was afterwards at St John's College, Cambridge, though he left the university without distinction. During travels in France he fell in love with the daughter of a surgeon of Blois, Annette Villon, by whom he had a daughter – a fact which only became generally known some forty years ago. Wordsworth, who had at first, like so many others, hailed the French Revolution, grew sickened at its excesses, and as age overtook him, he became increasingly conservative in outlook.

In 1795 Wordsworth first met Samuel Taylor Coleridge, and to the years which followed belong some of his best work including 'Lines Above Tintern Abbey'. He also began 'The Prelude' and this long poem, revised many times and not published until after his death, is at once his autobiography, the story of the evolution of a poet's mind, and an enduring testament.

In 1799 Wordsworth settled with his sister Dorothy at Grasmere, among the English lakes, a district which he left only to visit friends and for tours abroad. The beneficence of friends who believed in his genius and, as the years passed, his own increasing fame, ensured the settled life which he valued. At his finest, as in the 'Ode on Intimations of Immortality', his sonnet 'Upon Westminster Bridge', and in parts of his long poem 'The Excursion', he has rarely been equalled in his expression of the mystical relation between man and nature.

H. W. Pickersgill shows him as an elder statesman of letters.

I⊤ is not uncommon for a man to achieve reputation in one medium, and then to change to another which brings more lasting fame. It was so with Scott, whose early verse, founded upon his passion for tales and ballads of the Scots border, won wide acceptance. Yet it is by his novels that he is oftener remembered.

The son of an Edinburgh lawyer, Scott was himself called to the Bar, but the success of his verse, particularly 'The Lay of the Last Minstrel', decided him to give his best energies to letters, and he also took up a share in a printing and bookselling business. In 1814 he turned to novel writing, publishing *Waverley* anonymously, and following it by a succession of stories which only ended with his death. It was thirteen years before Scott officially acknowledged their authorship, by which time he had acquired Abbotsford, the Border home where he lived in splendid style, and had received a baronetcy; he had also assumed liability for the enormous sum of £130,000, due to the failure of the firm with which he was concerned. Scott shouldered his burdens with stoic fortitude, creditors being paid at his death with the sums realised on the sale of his copyrights.

Scott lived on a grand scale, and there is nothing petty in his work. His output was immense, and if, as a result, it is uneven in quality, such works as *Heart of Midlothian* are masterly.

Sir Henry Raeburn (1756-1823) painted Scott to general admiration.

THE year following Coleridge's death, Wordsworth, with whom he had once collaborated so memorably, wrote in his sorrow:

> Nor has the rolling year twice measured,
> From sign to sign its steadfast course,
> Since every mortal power of Coleridge
> Was frozen at its marvellous source;
> The rapt one, of the godlike forehead,
> The heaven-eyed creature sleeps in earth . . .

Coleridge was incomparable, as all who knew him agreed. Born in Devonshire, at Ottery St Mary, the youngest of thirteen children, he spent his boyhood, like Lamb, at Christ's Hospital, where his outstanding gifts were recognised. Much of his youth was spent in wandering: in England, Germany and Italy, and for a time he lived at Malta, acting as secretary to the Governor, Sir Alexander Ball, who had been one of Nelson's captains.

In 1798 *Lyrical Ballads* appeared, the volume, mainly by Wordsworth, which included Coleridge's 'The Rime of the Ancient Mariner'. 'Christabel' and 'Kubla Khan' were written at much the same time, though they were published later.

During his later life Coleridge succumbed to the habit of taking opium, but his mental powers, though sometimes clouded, remained magnificent. His *Biographia Literaria* was published in 1817, and his Notebooks, which are only now being produced in a scholar's edition, show him to have been one of the most universal geniuses this country has ever produced.

Peter Vandyke (1729-1796) once assistant to Sir Joshua Reynolds, painted Coleridge in 1795 and he has conveyed something of his compelling charm.

AMBITIOUS for fame, Southey believed he might attain a measure of immortality:

> My hopes are with the dead; anon
> My place with them will be,
> And I with them shall travel on
> Through all Infinity;
> Yet leaving here a name I trust
> That will not perish in the dust.

So wrote Southey, and as Laureate from 1813 until his death he had reason to hope that he might be remembered by his verse. Yet it is not as a poet that Southey is recalled, except for occasional pieces; it is for his prose, much of it written under pressure, and some of the best, such as his *Life of Nelson*, expanded from articles in journals.

Southey was educated at Westminster and Oxford. Caught up with early enthusiasms such as only Coleridge could generate, he became Coleridge's brother-in-law, and when the older man severed himself from his family, Southey assumed his friend's responsibilities, and from Greta Hall, Keswick, where he settled in 1803, he poured out a torrent of books to support a growing number of dependents. Like Scott, he wore himself out.

Southey's interest in the land and people of Portugal, originating in travels in that country, was maintained throughout his life, and his *History of Brazil* has at least some lasting value: moreover in the story of the Three Bears, which occurs in his miscellany, *The Doctor*, he added a new children's classic to a select and cherished repertory. Henry Edridge (1769-1821) drew him at the age of thirty.

JANE AUSTEN

1775-1817

JANE AUSTEN wrote some enchanting juvenilia and other fragments, but her fame rests upon six completed novels, which made her in her own sphere without rival in either sex. In order of their appearance, her principal books, *Sense and Sensibility*, *Pride and Prejudice*, *Mansfield Park*, *Emma* and *Northanger Abbey*, were published during her lifetime: only *Persuasion* was posthumous. There is no better picture of that rank of society which she knew from inside, but it is her wit, her irony and her character-drawing which win enthusiasts from every generation.

Jane Austen was born at Steventon in Hampshire, where her father was rector. There, and at Bath, South-ampton, Chawton and Winchester, with visits elsewhere, she lived out her uneventful life, observing, feeling, and recording, at first surreptitiously. 'The young lady,' said Scott, 'has a talent for describing the involvements of feelings and characters of ordinary life which is to me the most wonderful I have met with.' Nor can the charge be sustained that she was oblivious of the world events which were taking place around her. Two of her brothers rose to flag rank, and among her gallery of characters none are more vividly described than the naval and marine officers who figure so sympathetically in her pages.

Jane Austen's beloved sister Cassandra (1773-1845), to whom many of her letters are addressed, drew the only authenticated portrait. It is in pencil and water-colour, and it dates from about 1810, the year before the appearance of *Sense and Sensibility*.

ONE of the very last portraits painted by Hazlitt, which dates from 1804, was of his friend Lamb. It is in fancy dress, and the face is unforgettable. Not only does the portrait record Lamb vividly as he was in his comparative youth, but it shows how well Hazlitt could paint the sympathetic subject.

Although differing widely from him in character, Lamb's life had much the same quality as Johnson's. He suffered greatly; he loved his fellow men; he knew most of the better writers of his time; and he left behind him a residue of work which is remarkable, in particular the *Essays of Elia*, named after an Italian clerk formerly in South Sea House, which show an individuality and grace, often a playfulness of style entirely his own.

Lamb was a Londoner, and was educated at Christ's Hospital at the time when its star was Coleridge. At the age of eleven, his mother was killed by his sister Mary in a fit of insanity, and Lamb assumed charge of her until the end of his life; nursing her, caring for her, writing with her collaboration *Tales from Shakespeare* which was designed for children. Lamb was for years a city clerk, and a conscientious one, so that his writing was an accompaniment to the stress of winning daily bread. It included many contributions to the *London Magazine*.

Lamb used to say that he wrote for antiquity, so much did he admire old things. This was not true, but the remark has a typical flavour. To appreciate him, either as writer or man, is in a sense a touchstone of a reader's humanity.

HAZLITT had little luck with his friendships, being of a difficult nature, and none at all with his two marriages, but on his deathbed he said, to general surprise, that he had had a happy life. If this was indeed so, then it was because of his gift for seeing everything as if for the first time. He took enormous zest to everything he did, and in what he saw for himself he was rarely deceived.

The son of a Unitarian minister, Hazlitt was taken as a child to America. Later he spent much of his youth at Wem in Shropshire. When he launched out into life, he was fortunate in making acquaintance with Coleridge, Lamb, Wordsworth, and also with painters, for he set out to become an artist, and the portraits which survive by his hand show how well he might have done.

Hazlitt's writings divide into those on art and the drama, and miscellaneous essays, the best of which, such as 'On Going a Journey' are unsurpassed. There is also the literary criticism, which includes *Characters of Shakespeare's Plays* and *English Comic Writers*. Hazlitt's history, with his persistent adulation of Napoleon, is less happy, but *The Spirit of the Age* contains valuable assessments of his contemporaries, some of them caustic.

Hazlitt was drawn by various artists, though not with the success which he himself achieved. His picture is not in the best condition, but it is admirable self-portraiture.

LIKE Defoe before him, Thomas Quincey, who was a Manchester man, added a De to his name soon after he embarked on the adventure of letters. Even before he entered Worcester College, Oxford, he had begun a wandering existence, and he soon caught the habit of opium eating, whose slave he became. This led to his contributing a narrative as unique as it was honest, *The Confessions of an Opium Eater*, to the *London Magazine*. In 1807 De Quincey became known to Coleridge, Wordsworth and Southey and soon afterwards to Charles Lamb, who greatly valued his friendship. Later De Quincey settled at Grasmere and finally in Edinburgh, where he spent the latter part of his life.

De Quincey wrote a splendidly ornate prose, and his essays included 'On Murder as one of the Fine Arts', 'The English Mail Coach' and 'On the Knocking at the Gate in Macbeth', which show as unusual perception in matters of life in general as in purely literary criticism. The cadences of his elaborately piled-up sentences are enriched with splendid imagery, and sometimes give abiding expression to the visions seen in his more elaborate opium dreams. De Quincey also wrote perceptively about his friends, particularly Lamb, and as a talker he could produce, at his best, a torrent of eloquent opinion. Although unequal to the composition of a strictly ordered work of prose, his gifts were specially suited to the higher journalism where his essays and reflections were so welcome.

De Quincey was painted by Sir John Watson Gordon (1788-1864), his friend and contemporary.

1785-1866

A NOVELIST and to a lesser degree a poet, Peacock was the son of a well-to-do London merchant who, when he came to man's estate, found the paternal way of life uncongenial, and lived for some time on his private means. He wrote for pleasure – verse, and a series of satirical romances which continue to give pleasure – *Headlong Hall*, *Melincourt* and *Nightmare Abbey*. Then, belatedly, he entered the service of the East India Company, after which business engaged him, and his literary production fell away. *Crotchet Castle* and the much later *Gryll Grange* were his only remaining notable works, though two others, *Maid Marian*, which parodied the Robin Hood stories, and *The Misfortunes of Elphin*, which parodied the Arthurian Legends, have their flavour.

Peacock knew Shelley, and his memorials of the poet, which appeared in their final form long after both their deaths (they had originally been contributed to *Fraser's Magazine*) have much interest. Peacock's odd mixture of satire and romance, his narratives, diversified with song, are written in a light, piquant and alliterative style, the general scheme being the same in most of them. This consists of the gathering of a miscellaneous party of odd characters in a country house, enlivened by sparkling dialogue and absurd incidents.

In his official line, Peacock rose high, and it is Peacock the man of affairs who predominates in the portrait of 1858 by Henry Wallis (1830-1916).

A⊤ the age of ten Byron succeeded to a peerage, the
result of the immediate heir having been killed in action.
He was educated at Harrow and at Trinity College,
Cambridge, and soon discovered an exceptional facility
in writing verse. He worked his gift hard for the rest of
his life.

When he came of age, Byron began to travel abroad.
After he returned home he took his seat in the House of
Lords, and in the year 1812 the publication of the early
cantos of his travel narrative, *Childe Harold's Pilgrimage*,
enraptured London. Byron awoke, as he said, to find
himself famous. In 1815 he married an heiress, Anne
Isabella Milbanke, but separated within a year, amid
scandal. He then went abroad for good, living in Venice,
Ravenna, Pisa and elsewhere. In 1823 he joined actively
in the movement for the liberation of Greece from the
yoke of Turkey, and he died of fever at Missolonghi in
the following year. Thomas Phillips (1770-1845) painted
a portrait commemorative of the cause for which Byron
gave his life.

In his verse, particularly in *Don Juan*, his longest
poem, Byron showed himself vigorous and free thinking,
the enemy of cant in all its forms. His descriptive scenes
are romantic, like the character of his heroes, and his
high spirits, well shown in the early 'English Bards and
Scotch Reviewers' and in the much later 'Beppo' rarely
failed him. His letters, written in a plain and racy prose,
were as vivid as his verse. Byron lived a disordered life,
but as an artist he was increasingly serious, though never
solemn.

THE son of a Sussex landowner, Shelley was sent down from University College, Oxford, in 1811 for publishing a pamphlet on *The Necessity of Atheism*. During the course of the next year he married, wandered about the country, and began writing serious poetry, his first considerable work, 'Queen Mab', dating from 1818. His marriage was not enduring, and he soon attached himself to Mary, daughter of William Godwin (1756-1836) the philosopher. He married her after the suicide of his first wife.

Shelley left England for good in 1818. He lived henceforward in Italy, and in Rome he wrote two of his more outstanding works, 'The Cenci' and 'Prometheus Unbound'. In 1820 he removed to Venice in company with Byron. A year later he wrote 'Adonais', a lament for Keats, for whose work he had the highest admiration. After a short stay at Pisa he went to Lerici on the Gulf of Spezia, and was drowned in a sailing accident. His body was cast ashore a fortnight later and burnt on a pyre in the presence of Byron, Leigh Hunt (1784-1859) and Edward John Trelawny (1792-1881). His ashes were preserved and buried in the Protestant Cemetery at Rome near those of Keats, whose poems had been found on his body.

Shelley was a lyric poet of the highest powers, and 'The Cenci' showed that he could have extended his gifts to the drama. In character gentle and generous, he was a born rebel, and did not take kindly to responsibility as the conventional understand it. Amelia Curran (*d.* 1847) captured something of the poet's magic in her portrait.

CARLYLE was born at Ecclefechan, in Dumbartonshire, and studied at Annan Academy and Edinburgh University, to which he travelled ninety miles on foot. After a spell as a tutor, he began the serious study of German history and literature, one which continued throughout his life. At the age of just over thirty he married Jane Baillie Welsh, a lady of strong character, shrewd wit, and one of the best letter writers in the language. The marriage, though it had varied fortunes, partly due to Carlyle's absorption in his work, lasted forty years, and Carlyle wrote little of importance after his wife's death.

After removal to Chelsea in 1834, Carlyle completed a work on the French Revolution on which he had been engaged for some years, the first volume of which had been accidentally burnt. Publication established his reputation as historian and, to some extent, seer. When he turned his attention to current problems, as in *Past and Present* (1843) he showed contempt for many of the teachings of political economy and for democratic nostrums. Salvation, so he believed, was to be sought in a return to medieval conditions and the rule of the strong just man, who was not to be got by popular election. As the spokesman for and interpreter of heroes, Carlyle followed up an earlier book on this subject with a study of Oliver Cromwell's speeches and letters and by a history of Frederick the Great which took him fifteen years. Carlyle evolved a prose style which, though imitation invites disaster, is at its best remarkable. Walter Greaves (*b. c.* 1841) painted Carlyle during his last years.

Painted about 1879
W. Greaves.

SHORT as his life was, Keats lived long enough to leave behind him poems and letters showing a mind in flower, wonderfully gifted.

At the age of fifteen Keats was apprenticed to a surgeon at Edmonton. Five years later he began to walk the London hospitals. The life did not much attract him, and he turned increasingly to letters. His first book of poems fell flat, and his second, *Endymion*, was savagely attacked, when it appeared in 1818, by *Blackwood* and the *Quarterly*. Two years later appeared *Lamia and other Poems*, a collection which included 'Isabella', 'The Eve of St Agnes', 'Hyperion' and the odes 'To a Nightingale' and 'On a Grecian Urn', all of which had been produced within a period of about eighteen months. By the end of that time, Keats' health, which had been sapped by consumption, was almost shattered, and he was, moreover, handicapped by narrow means and saddened by unfulfilled love. In 1820 he set out, accompanied by Joseph Severn (1793-1879), who painted the best known portrait, on a journey to Italy from which he never returned. He died in Rome, where his tomb, together with that of Shelley, became an object of pilgrimage.

The principal characteristics of Keats's verse, its sensuous imagination, its absorption with the idea of beauty, and its descriptive power, are matched in his letters by a rare blend of sympathy, thought and observation. Keats won the admiration of such friends as Lamb, Hazlitt and Leigh Hunt (1784-1859) who knew how to value gifts mourned by Shelley in *Adonais*.

61 THOMAS BABINGTON MACAULAY

1800-1859

IF Gibbon marshalled and surveyed the later Roman Empire, Macaulay brought the history of his own country before the general reader. He had the power to make the past as enthralling as fiction, and could extend his narrative gift to historical verse.

Macaulay was the son of Zachary Macaulay, philanthropist and anti-slaver. He went to Trinity College, Cambridge, read law, and became a pillar of the *Edinburgh Review*. A brilliant conversationalist, with an exceptional memory, Macaulay was soon attracted to politics; still later he went to India as a member of the Supreme Council, on which he exerted his influence in favour of the choice of an English rather than an oriental type of education. When he returned to London and to literature and politics, he was given office as Secretary of State for War, and later as Paymaster of the Forces.

The *Lays of Ancient Rome* appeared in 1842, and in the year following a collection of *Essays*, mainly in biography and history, which enjoyed a wide circulation, and the best of which continue to be read. His last and most substantial work was a *History of England from the Accession of James II*, of which the first two volumes appeared in 1848, and two succeeding ones seven years later. This was never completed, but enough appeared to establish the author as one of those men who could clothe a past epoch with life, and portray the principal characters in the round. In 1857 the author was raised to the peerage. He was painted by Sir Francis Grant (1803-1878).

THE mainspring of the Tractarian Movement within
the Church of England, one of its purposes being to
revive knowledge of that Church's historic past, Newman
in time left its fold. He made his spiritual pilgrimage the
subject of his greatest work, *Apologia pro Vita Sua*.

Educated privately and at Trinity College, Oxford,
Newman became a Fellow of Oriel, and at the age of
twenty-seven was presented to the vicarage of St Mary's,
Oxford, where his sermons, musical in delivery, intellectual in content and at times controversial, drew many.
In 1841 he argued the compatibility of the articles of the
Church of England with Roman Catholic theology, and
found himself under a ban. Two years later he resigned
his living, and in 1845 he was received into the Church
of Rome, later in life becoming Cardinal of St George in
Velabro.

Newman's principle work of literature, his *Apologia*,
was written in answer to a charge Charles Kingsley
(1819-1875) had made, in *Macmillan's Magazine*, that
Newman did not consider truth to be a necessary virtue.
It is an exposition, written with the utmost simplicity
but with a wealth of argument and illustration, of the
evolution of his thought. Newman also wrote *The Dream
of Gerontius*, set to music by Sir Edward Elgar (1857-
1934), a dramatic monologue on the theme of the just
soul leaving the body at death, also a number of hymns.
The hymns include 'Lead Kindly Light', which he composed, during his early travels, on an orange boat
between Palermo and Marseilles.

Newman's influence was personal as well as literary,
and, apart from his theology, his 'The Idea of a University Defined' has lasting importance. George Richmond (1809-1896), once a pupil of Blake, made a chalk
drawing of Newman in his Oxford years.

BORROW was educated at Edinburgh High School and later at Norwich, after which he was articled to a solicitor. It was a line which did not suit him. He helped in compiling the *Newgate Calendar* of celebrated crimes, and then embarked on a wandering life in England, France, Germany, Russia, Spain and the East, studying the languages of the countries he visited, compiling a dictionary of the Gipsy language, and translating the New Testament into Manchu.

In Russia and Spain, Borrow acted as agent for the British and Foreign Bible Society, and in the latter country acted at one stage as correspondent of *The Times*. Finally he settled near Oulton Broad in Suffolk, where he became known for open if sometimes eccentric hospitality.

Borrow was a philologist of rank, but his best known books are a blend of gypsy lore, fiction, and travel-autobiography. They include *The Bible in Spain*, recalling his adventures in the years between 1835 and 1840; *Lavengro*, notable for the character of the Flaming Tinman; the *Romany Rye*, which is a sequel to *Lavengro* (Romany Rye in gypsy language signifies 'Gipsy Gentlemen'); and *Wild Wales*. Borrow's books are aglow with the spirit of 'the wind on the heath', and are remarkable for picturesque description of vagabond life. His appearance and character were almost as remarkable as the life he had led, and his writing, whether fact or romance, never lacked flavour.

Borrow was painted by his brother, John Thomas Borrow (1800-1833), in his earlier years.

BENJAMIN DISRAELI, novelist and man of letters, became in course of time Earl of Beaconsfield, statesman and Conservative Prime Minister: but politics were always an element in his writing, while the novelist's Parliamentary career had in itself some flavour of fiction.

Vivian Grey, published when the author was twenty-two, started him on a writing career. Other novels soon followed, always with a social implication beneath their surface glitter. In 1837 Disraeli entered Parliament as Member for Maidstone. He was laughed at in the House for his dandified appearance and lack of conventional background, but he soon made himself respected. Later novels, *Coningsby* and *Sybil*, both included material which derived directly from his political experiences, and *Sybil* drew the very real distinction between what the author called the 'Two Nations' – the rich and the poor.

Disraeli's rise to office absorbed most of his energy between the publication of *Tancred*, in 1847, and 1870, when he published *Lothair*. He was Prime Minister for ten months in 1868 and again from 1874 to 1880, when he became not merely the first servant of the Crown but the close friend of Queen Victoria.

Disraeli's works contain valuable commentary – they also depict types and show the motives which actuate them. Real people figure among his characters, thinly disguised, but usually drawn with a kindly humour.

Sir John Everett Millais (1829-1896) painted the best known portrait of a man in whom was blended the power to please and the will to power.

TENNYSON

UPON Wordsworth's death in 1850, Alfred Tennyson succeeded him as Poet Laureate. The qualifications of the holder matched the office he was given, for few have equalled him in rising to the public occasion. He had recently published *In Memoriam* – a sustained poem-series to the memory of his friend Arthur Hallam: within two years he had written the *Ode on the Death of the Duke of Wellington*, one of the best celebratory poems of the nineteenth century.

Tennyson's father was a Lincolnshire parson, and the poet, before going to Trinity College, Cambridge, had been educated at the Grammar School at Louth. From comparatively early years his output was steady, various and remarkably even. His more ambitious poems include *The Idylls of the King*, based on Sir Thomas Malory's Arthurian cycle, and *The Princess*. He also poured out a succession of lyrics, ballads and verse dramas which not only pleased the taste of his time, but which are still read with pleasure. He was one of the few poets popular enough to live by their verse, so much so that the offer of a peerage in 1884 caused him no embarrassment. Tennyson was universally revered, and when he died, in his 84th year, he was given a public funeral and burial in Westminster Abbey.

Tennyson was frequently painted after he had grown a beard, and had become seer and sage. Samuel Laurence (1812-1884), who knew him in his earlier years, shows a man not yet corresponding to the Victorian idea of the typical poet.

ONE of the best letter-writers of any age, Fitzgerald is remembered through his correspondence with an friendship for such men as Carlyle, Tennyson and Thackeray, and for his translation of the Rubaiyat of Omar Khayyam. This rendering of a twelfth-century Persian poem, celebrating the moment as it passes, escaped notice when it first appeared. Revival of interest came almost by chance, but attention has continued, and it is as much quoted as any work in the language.

Fitzgerald was at Trinity College, Cambridge, with Tennyson. Afterwards he lived mainly in Suffolk. He married the daughter of Bernard Barton, a poet friend of Charles Lamb, but the union did not last, and Fitzgerald settled down to make much of a long life, translating authors of whom he grew fond. His abilities were far beyond those of the literal renderer, a remark which applies almost as much to his versions of Aeschylus, Sophocles and Calderon as to his Persian classic. In later life he collected material for a Dictionary of the *dramatis personae* in the letters of Madame de Sevigné.

Fitzgerald is one of the many writers whose influence cannot be judged by their output. He was a notable critic, and his leisure enabled him to serve his friends. His retiring habits prevented him from sitting for a full-scale portrait. A miniature, based on a photograph by Cade of Ipswich, preserves some record of his appearance.

THE daughter of a Unitarian minister, Elizabeth Gaskell, as she became on her marriage, was brought up by an aunt at Knutsford, Cheshire, the scene of her best known picture of the social life of her time, *Cranford*, and a place which also figures in her longer novel, *Wives and Daughters*.

Elizabeth Gaskell's husband was minister of a chapel in Manchester, and as the result of her knowledge and experience in the industrial north she wrote *Mary Barton*, which was critical of employers typical of the age. By the time she came to write *North and South*, serialised by Dickens in *Household Words*, slightly better conditions were beginning to prevail, though the picture was still grim. In all Mrs Gaskell's work, except for the delightful *Cranford*, there is a critical attitude towards social problems, and a deep seriousness of intention.

In addition to her novels, which include *Sylvia's Loves* and the unfinished *Wives and Daughters*, Mrs Gaskell published in 1857 her *Life of Charlotte Brontë*. It is one of the classic biographies in the language, written from immediate knowledge, soon after her fellow-novelist's death, and with all the necessary equipment. It is one of those books where author and subject are perfectly matched, and it is difficult to see how it could be better done.

George Richmond (1809-1896) made a chalk drawing of Mrs Gaskell in 1851, at the time when she was contributing *Cranford* to *Household Words*.

WILLIAM MAKEPEACE THACKERAY was born in India, and at the age of six was sent to England to school, first to Chiswick and then to Charterhouse, where he was unhappy. He went later to Trinity College, Cambridge, did not take a degree, but made lasting friends in Tennyson and Fitzgerald. Travel abroad included a meeting with Goethe (1749-1832) at Weimar, and a period when he settled in Paris with the idea of becoming an artist. In 1837, the year of Queen Victoria's accession, he returned to England, where he began that career of writing which ended only with his death. He had dissipated a comfortable inheritance, and he had to write to live.

Thackeray's private life was saddened by the insanity of his wife, a tragedy which occurred after they had been six years together. Of his many novels *Vanity Fair*, which was issued in monthly numbers in the years 1847-48, has achieved most lasting favour, particularly for the character of Becky Sharp, the successful adventuress who holds the stage whenever she appears. *Pendennis*, *Esmond*, *The Newcomes* and *The Virginians* are among his best work. In each of these books Thackeray exercised his gift of bringing history to life, and the ability to draw convincing characters, particularly from the higher ranks of society.

Thackeray became first editor of *The Cornhill*. He ended his days with a double success. He established his magazine triumphantly, and he was recognised as a novelist second only to Dickens in stature. Samuel Laurence (1812-1884) drew Thackeray in what would have been, from the nature of his life, a characteristic attitude.

IN scope and vitality, and in the creation of enduring characters, Dickens has no rival among English novelists. Seen during his own life-time mainly as entertainer and social commentator, with emphasis on the entertainer, Dickens has only lately been studied as a literary craftsman. His work was largely conditioned by the fact that he wrote with the press waiting. Like Shakespeare, he was prepared to adapt his material (even at the last minute) to what his audience required, so that there is no element whatever, in his novels or his journalism, of art for art's sake. Dickens was a shrewd man who in his later years exploited his gifts as a reader of his own stories. He worked himself so hard that he shortened his own life.

Dickens's father was a government clerk who was always in debt, and the boy's earlier years included a spell in a blacking factory. In 1832 he became a reporter of debates in the House of Commons, and from then onwards his life was one of ceaseless activity as journalist, novelist and editor. In 1850 he started the weekly periodical *Household Words*, which was succeeded nine years later by *All the Year Round*.

Dickens paid many visits abroad, including two to America, and until the last was at work on his novels. These, *The Pickwick Papers*, *Oliver Twist*, *David Copperfield*, *Dombey and Son* and a long succession, are still, in his own phrase 'household words'.

W. P. Frith (1819-1909), a highly successful contemporary, painted Dickens at his desk, the calendar reminding him that a new instalment of his current story was due at the printer.

Victoria and Albert Museum : Crown copyright

THE son of a clerk in the Bank of England, Browning was privately educated. He first visited Italy at the age of twenty-two, and ever afterwards that country and its history became a predominant interest in his life and in his poetry. Browning's *Paracelsus* was the first volume to attract the notice of Carlyle, Wordsworth and others, and in 1837 his tragedy, *Strafford*, was performed at Covent Garden.

At the age of thirty-four Browning rescued Elizabeth Barrett from the clutches of a morbidly possessive father, married her, and lived for most of the remainder of his life in Italy. Elizabeth died in 1861 with a secure name as a poet in her own right. Seven years later there appeared Browning's longest and in some respects his best poem, *The Ring and the Book*, based upon an actual murder as related in an old parchment-covered volume that Browning picked up one day in a Florentine market stall. It is an extraordinary mixture of prolixity, technical virtuosity and genuine dramatic effect.

Browning was at times notably obscure, which led to the formation of societies to study his work, but his more colloquial manner – well shown in his dramatic monologues – helped towards a greater freedom of expression in Victorian and later verse. Poems such as 'Rabbi Ben Ezra', 'The Pied Piper of Hamelin' and 'A Grammarian's Funeral', whose meaning is self-evident, are proof that when he thought clearly he could also write with effect. Michele Gordigiani (1830-1909) painted the poet in 1858 when he was at the height of his contemporary fame.

ANTHONY TROLLOPE created the county of Barsetshire, its cathedral town, its market towns and villages, its churches, manors and houses, and peopled it with characters so actual that no effort is needed on the part of a reader to believe he is reading the living truth. The saintly Mr Harding, the abominable Mrs Proudie, ruler of Bishop and diocese, the four-square, worldly Archdeacon Grantly, show that Trollope had the sympathetic intuition and the touch which quickens character. He himself was convinced that his Palliser political series were his best work, but later generations have preferred Barsetshire.

Trollope was a busy Post Office official who travelled widely on the Queen's business, and a civil servant of capacity and consequence. He lived a full life, and, after an unhappy boyhood, a happy and successful one. When he came to write his *Autobiography* – published posthumously – he made what seemed at the time a cardinal mistake: he told his readers just how many thousand pounds his books made him – £70,000 down to 1879 – and robbed the novelist's craft of all the mumbo-jumbo with which more high-flown craftsmen tried to surround it. It was, it appeared, all done by hard, regular work. Trollope's reputation slumped as the result of his honesty, but posterity finds the *Autobiography* one of the more enthralling works of its kind, and is enchanted to learn that Trollope killed off Mrs Proudie as the result of conversation overheard at his club.

Samuel Laurence (1812-1884), who also portrayed Trollope's hero Thackeray, painted the novelist in 1865, when the Barsetshire series was drawing towards its close.

.

ABOUT the year 1833 Patrick Branwell Brontë (1817-1848) painted a portrait of his three surviving sisters which, from its associations, is as precious as Cassandra's version of Jane Austen. Though he left little behind him but this, it has kept him in remembrance.

Haworth, high on the Yorkshire moors, had as its perpetual curate, between 1820 and 1861, an Irishman, Patrick Prunty, who changed his name after Nelson had been given the Sicilian dukedom of Brontë. This clergyman, whose wife died in 1821, had five daughters and a son. Three of the daughters were women of genius. Charlotte, the longest lived (though even she never reached forty), became author of *Jane Eyre* and other novels. Emily wrote *Wuthering Heights* and some splendid poetry, while Anne wrote *Agnes Grey* and *The Tenant of Wildfell Hall*. The two elder daughters died unknown to fame, and Branwell made nothing of his life.

In 1846 there appeared a volume of verse by Currer, Ellis and Acton Bell, the pseudonyms of Charlotte, Emily and Anne. In the following year, Charlotte published *Jane Eyre*, Emily published *Wuthering Heights*, her only novel, and Anne *Agnes Grey*, the first of her two works of fiction. The event of three sisters publishing lasting books in the same year is unique in literature: so is the interest which the Brontës have excited ever since.

ANNE
1820-1849

EMILY
1818-1848

CHARLOTTE
1816-1855

IN a century when the seer and prophet came into his own, Ruskin could challenge even Carlyle in the vehemence of his expression, the range of his interests, and the influence of his personality.

The son of a well-to-do wine merchant, Ruskin had no formal schooling. Travel, and his years at Christ Church, Oxford, where he won the Newdigate Prize for verse, were formative influences upon his thought. His first important work was *Modern Painters*, the first volume of which appeared in 1843, the series being continued until 1860. Ruskin was the foremost champion of J. M. W. Turner (1775-1851), a very great artist whose later works had been misunderstood. Turner neither needed nor greatly valued Ruskin's championship, but it gave the young critic splendid opportunities for the exercise of his richly mellifluous prose style. Over the years this was devoted to architecture, drawing – Ruskin himself was a draughtsman of the highest skill – economics, war, social reform, commentaries which appeared with titles such as 'Unto this Last', 'Munera Pulveris', 'Sesame and Lilies', 'Time and Tide by Weare and Tyne'. They were not all calculated to entice, but they are invariably worth reading.

Ruskin became the first Slade Professor of the Fine Arts at Oxford, where his lectures attracted much attention, and he also benefited Oxford by endowing a drawing school. George Richmond (1809-1896) made a delicate study of Ruskin in middle life.

Mary Ann Evans: 1819-1880

'GEORGE ELIOT', the pen name of Mary Ann Evans, came to be adopted by the daughter of a Warwickshire estate agent who discovered a gift for letters. She began her literary life with a translation of Strauss's *Life of Jesus*, published in 1846. Four years later she started contributing to the *Westminster Review*, of which she became assistant editor. In 1854 she formed a close association with George Henry Lewes (1817-1878), philosopher and authority on Goethe. This lasted until Lewes's death, when Mary Ann married their mutual friend John Cross.

George Eliot was a thoughtful and impressive journalist, but she is remembered for her novels, particularly for *Adam Bede*, with its notable scenes of rural life, for *The Mill on the Floss*, with its setting in Lincolnshire, and above all for *Middlemarch*, which appeared in 1871 and contains extremely subtle characterisation and valuable social commentary.

George Eliot was the most intellectual woman writer of her time. Capable of humour and pathos, and of closely observed character drawing, particularly of the farming community of the Midland counties, her novels carry a deep conviction of the purifying effect of suffering. Her wide and varied learning is reflected in her essays, which were collected as *Impressions of Theophrastus Such*.

The novelist was drawn in middle life by Sir Frederick Burton (1816-1900).

A son of Thomas Arnold (1795-1842), headmaster of Rugby, Matthew Arnold was educated at Rugby, Winchester and Balliol College, Oxford, where an early poem won him the Newdigate Prize. No one has ever loved Oxford better, or savoured more its countryside, a fact reflected in his best-known poem, *The Scholar Gipsy*, which appeared in 1853.

Arnold became a Fellow of Oriel College, then, after a spell as secretary to Lord Lansdowne, he was appointed an Inspector of Schools, a post which he held from 1851 for over thirty years. From 1857 until 1867 he was also Professor of Poetry at Oxford, where he was able to deliver pronouncements on poetry and criticism at a time when he himself was writing original work of distinction.

After 1865 Arnold's production was mainly prose, his *Essays in Criticism* (1865 and 1888) making criticism a matter of the widest scope, extending it to an attack on the 'philistinism' and 'provinciality' which he believed to prevail in the England of his day, an idea with which many thoughtful people agreed.

Arnold's *Culture and Anarchy*, a commentary on English social and political life, was perhaps his most important contribution to the thought of his age. Arnold did not much like the world as he saw it, but his outlook, particularly on education, was constructive, and the best of his poetry has an assured place in the English canon.

No painted portrait caught the essence of Arnold's character quite so well as a photograph taken in his later years.

THE son of William Collins, R.A. (1787-1847), a landscape painter whose life he wrote, William Wilkie Collins was called to the Bar, but soon relinquished the law for literature. Millais painted him in 1850, the year in which he published his first novel, *Antonina*, an historical romance, but Collins soon found his true field in the story of contemporary life, his power lying in the construction of a skilful plot, which not merely holds the attention of the reader, but sustains his curiosity.

Collins's two best novels were *The Woman in White*, published in 1860 by his friend Dickens as a serial in *All the Year Round*, a mystery tale in which the device is used of telling the story by means of several characters in succession, and *The Moonstone*, which appeared in 1868.

Owing to the development of the genre over the past century, and the skill which writers of great talent have brought to it, *The Moonstone* has importance as a landmark, for it was in its pages that one of the first detectives appeared in fiction – Sergeant Cuff. The story is concerned with the theft of a diamond, once set in the forehead of an image of the Indian moon-god.

Although later writers have surpassed him in ingenuity and technical knowledge, Collins was in a real sense prophetic of a large and attractive succession. He and Sir Arthur Conan Doyle (1859-1930) were among the founding fathers of the crime story.

Collins was painted as a young man by Sir John Everett Millais (1829-1896).

DANTE GABRIEL, William Michael (1829-1919), and their sister Christina (1830-1894), all of whom wrote poetry, were the children of Gabriele Rossetti, an Italian scholar who came to England in 1824 and was made Professor of Italian at King's College, London: their mother, Frances Poldori, was half Italian.

Dante Gabriel was educated at King's College School, and began training as a painter, being contemporary with William Holman Hunt (1827-1910), Millais and others of that pre-Raphaelite School who united to resist current conventions by returning to art forms as they supposed them to have existed before the time of Raphael. As a protest, the Movement had a vitalising influence on art and letters, work being produced of great beauty of detail and colour.

Rossetti's earlier fame came through his painting, but he wrote poetry most of his adult life. He married Eleanor Siddon, a girl of striking looks, in 1860; and when she died, two years later, he buried the manuscript of his poems with her. These were later disinterred and were published in 1870. Rossetti was also a translator from Italian, French and German.

Rossetti's pencil self-portrait dates from 1847, at the time when some of his best-known poems, such as 'The Blessed Damozel', were appearing in *The Germ*, the magazine of the Movement to which he belonged.

THE son of Melchizedeck Meredith, a naval tailor at Portsmouth whose character inspired an early novel, *Evan Harrington*, George Meredith was sent to school locally, and later to the Moravian School of Neuwied. Settling in London, he contributed to Dickens's *Household Words*, and in 1849 he married Mary Ellen Nicholls, a widowed daughter of Thomas Love Peacock. Some years after his first wife's death Meredith married Marie Vulliamy and lived with her many years in Flint Cottage on Box Hill, Dorking, where he wrote poems and novels, and where, as reader to Messrs Chapman and Hall, he acted as literary midwife to a host of lesser writers.

In his earlier years Meredith was a close friend of Rossetti and other leading pre-Raphaelites, but his poem-sequence, *Modern Love*, intimate and vital, owes little to their influence. Meredith thought of his novels as high comedy, which they sometimes were. The element is seen at its best in *The Egoist*, which appeared in 1879 and was described as 'a comedy of narrative', the hero, Sir Willoughby Patterne, rich and handsome, suffering from selfishness and conceit, leading to inevitable humiliations. Meredith had earlier published *The Ordeal of Richard Feverel* and *Beauchamp's Career*, both of which had considerable success.

Meredith was thought of as a sage by his own generation. His output in fiction, verse and criticism was large, considering his other preoccupations, and the finest of his verse has lasted better than his fiction. Like so many of the Victorians he was painted by his Surrey friend and neighbour, G. F. Watts (1817-1904).

ALICE IN WONDERLAND, including Alice herself, the White Rabbit, the Duchess and the Cheshire Cat, the Dormouse and the treacle-well, the Mad Hatter and the March Hare, the King and Queen of Hearts and the Mock Turtle, entered literature by way of Lewis Carroll. They are there to stay. So are Tweedledum and Tweedledee, Humpty Dumpty, the Jabberwock, the Walrus and the Carpenter, creatures in *Through the Looking Glass*, one of few successful sequels. Alice made her first appearance in 1865, her second seven years later.

The author of this sublime nonsense was a mathematician, christened Charles Lutwidge Dodgson. He was a product of Arnold's Rugby and of Christ Church, Oxford, where he became a don and lectured on his more serious subject from 1855 to 1881.

Lewis Carroll had the luck to find a perfect illustrator in Sir John Tenniel (1820-1914), and in addition to his Alice books he published *The Hunting of the Snark* in 1876, a poem about the elusive creature who turned out to be a Boojum.

Lewis Carroll is cherished by young and old among those who speak the English language. Harry Furniss (1854-1925) drew a caricature which was said to be something like him – certainly a more formal portrait at Christ Church conveys little but the mathematician. Dodgson was a shy man, with rather a stammer, and he never married. His success with children was, as a rule, instantaneous, and if they carried a sense of the ridiculous into grown-up life, they had a lasting friend in the author.

Lewis Carroll

from Some Victorian
Men

WILLIAM MORRIS was a practical idealist who strove to improve the taste of his age. 'What we like', wrote Ruskin, 'determines what we are.' Morris, who agreed with him, set out to revolutionise what men liked, at the outset by reference to what he considered to have been the enchanting Middle Ages.

Morris was born at Walthamstow and went to Marlborough and Exeter College, Oxford. He was then articled to an architect, afterwards becoming a painter and a friend of some of the principal pre-Raphaelites, with whom he founded a manufacturing and decorating firm. As a writer, his first important book was *The Defence of Guenevere and Other Poems*, which appeared in 1858. He continued to write verse and prose for the rest of his life, and he made a special study of the Icelandic sagas, which were the source of some of his most deeply felt work.

Among many other activities, Morris tried to revive the illumination of manuscripts – two of *Omar Khayyam* are among the best examples: more importantly, he started the Kelmscott Press, for which he designed type and decorations, his Chaucer being among the noblest looking books of the century. Morris's thought led him towards Socialism, for he was not merely a dreamer, but a man of practical aims. His vigorous countenance, rubicund in colouring, was a favourite subject with artists, among them G. F. Watts (1817-1904).

BOTH the Samuel Butlers who figure in English literature were satirists. The author of *Hudibras* (1612-1680) flayed the hypocrites of his time. His Victorian namesake, in his novel *The Way of All Flesh*, exposed the tyrannical religious parent so pervasive in the earlier nineteenth century.

Samuel Butler was a clergyman's son, his grandfather, Dr Samuel Butler (1774-1839) being Headmaster of Shrewsbury and later Bishop of Lichfield. Educated at Shrewsbury and at St John's College, Cambridge, Butler, who had been intended by his father for the church, went to New Zealand to breed sheep, returning to England in 1864 to settle in London at Clifford's Inn.

In 1872 Butler's satire *Erewhon* (Nowhere) appeared. It was the pithiest satire of its day. Illness was treated as a crime, and machinery was shown to have developed to such a point that it had to be abolished. *Erewhon* was Butler's most successful book, but he wrote many others apart from his novel, many of them controversial. *Life and Habit* discussed the theory of evolution: *Alps and Sanctuaries* told of adventures in Piedmont and the Ticino. Butler had the notion that the *Odyssey* was written by a woman, and he himself translated both the Homeric epics into prose. He left behind him Notebooks of attractive breadth of interest which were edited by his friend Henry Festing Jones.

Butler infused life into everything he touched. He painted and composed music, and he took nothing, except himself, for granted. He was painted by Charles Gogin (*fl.* 1871-1896).

TENNYSON said of Swinburne that he was 'a reed through which all things blow into music.' There are few poets more mellifluous, swifter in the pace of their narrative, or so ardent in metrical experiment.

Swinburne, born of aristocratic parents, was at Eton and at Balliol College, Oxford, though he went down without a degree. After leaving the university he lived for a time in Italy, and later in Chelsea where he became a friend of Rossetti and Meredith. Recognition of his calibre as a poet came after the publication of *Atalanta in Calydon* in 1865. In the same year he published the first of a series of poetic tragedies, better suited to the study than the stage. Over the next forty years his output was steady, his prose including much enthusiastic criticism, and a defence of the pre-Raphaelites, who had been attacked by Robert Buchanan (1841-1901) in a work called *The Fleshly School of Poetry*.

If Swinburne sang, he also shocked, his *Poems and Ballads* (1866) coming under such censure that the original publisher, Moxon, quailed and handed book and author over to John Camden Hotten, founder of the firm of Chatto and Windus. Swinburne's excesses had in the end to be restrained, and for the last thirty years of his life he was the companion of Theodore Watts Dunton (1832-1914), living at the Pines, Putney.

Dante Gabriel Rossetti (1828-1882) caught something of Swinburne's flaming personality in a portrait which is a memorable token of their friendship.

WHEN Hardy was born at Upper Bockhampton, Dorset, the neighbourhood was still pervaded with memories of the days when south England had been an armed camp, preparing to face a French invasion which never came. The shadow of Napoleon haunts some of his poems and stories; his era is the background for some of the novels, and the Napoleonic Age is the subject of his long and ironic epic-drama, *The Dynasts*.

Hardy's father was a builder, and he himself practised architecture in early life. According to his own classification, his many novels group themselves into those of Environment, such as *The Woodlanders, Tess of the D'Urbervilles* and *Jude the Obscure*; Romances and Fantasies, of which one of the best is *The Trumpet Major*; and Novels of Ingenuity, such as *A Laodicean*, the least successful kind.

Hardy won an immense reputation for his fiction, his Wessex countryside being richer, wider and far more tragically beautiful than Trollope's four-square Barchester: but for much of his long life he was also writing lyric poetry and this, at its best, is as memorable as any work of its time.

Although his outlook was fundamentally sombre, Hardy's loving observation of his own countryside, and of nature generally, was apparent in everything he wrote. Augustus John (1878-1961), a man as distinguished in art as Hardy in letters, painted Hardy in his later years, and expressed something of his quiet majesty.

HENRY JAMES was born in New York of Scots and Irish ancestry, his father being a follower of Swedenborg (1688-1772), the philosopher and mystic, and his elder brother William (1842-1910), a philosopher and psychologist.

James felt himself drawn towards the older society of Europe, and, having the means to do so, he travelled extensively before settling in England to a life of the dedicated artist in prose. Forty years later, in the stress of the First World War, he became naturalised, having for some years made his home at Rye.

James was a close observer of people, within the restricted range of his own experience, and his immense sequence of novels and stories present meticulous analyses of states of mind. Sometimes the mainspring of such action as there is lies in the contrast between the habits of the Old World and the New. A convoluted manner of expression was James's habit both in writing and speech. He made use of a Chinese nest of parentheses, as one critic remarked, and there was a grain of truth in the comment that he resembled a hippopotamus trying to pick up a pea. Among James's best known novels are *The Ambassador*, *Daisy Miller*, *What Maisie Knew*, *The American*, and *The Golden Bowl*. He also wrote a number of plays, which failed during his lifetime, though some of his fiction has since been adapted for the stage with great effect. His sinister story, *The Turn of the Screw*, is one of the best of its kind in the language.

James was painted in 1913 by John Singer Sargent (1856-1925), an American by race who also worked long in England.

THE case of Gerard Manley Hopkins is singular in English letters. His brief life, most of it dedicated to the Roman Catholic priesthood, began and ended in the Victorian era. His principal literary correspondent, Robert Bridges (1844-1930), Poet Laureate from 1913 until his death, encouraged him by his friendship, though he never fully understood Hopkins's work, and it is only within the last forty years that he has been appreciated as one of the most original minds of his time.

Hopkins was educated at Highgate School and at Balliol College, Oxford, where he came under the influence of Benjamin Jowett (1817-1893), most famous of its Masters, and of Walter Pater (1839-1894). Hopkins entered the Jesuit Novitiate in 1868, and in 1884 was appointed to the Chair of Greek at Dublin University.

No verse by Hopkins was published in book form during his lifetime, but his work was collected by Bridges, who issued an edition in 1918. Further poems were printed some twelve years later.

Hopkins's letters to Bridges, which are vital to the full understanding of his experiments and aims, appeared between 1935 and 1938, and his Notebooks have also been edited. He added meticulous draughtsmanship to his other gifts, but self-portraiture was not in his line, and the best likeness which survives is by his aunt, Anne Eleanor Hopkins (*fl.* 1850-1860) which shows him as a very young man.

ROBERT LOUIS STEVENSON's father was Engineer to the Board of Northern Lighthouses, and he was born in Edinburgh. At the University he studied engineering, but gave it up for the law. Forced to travel for reasons of health, Stevenson made tours in Belgium and France, commemorated in *An Inland Voyage* and *Travels with a Donkey in the Cevennes*. In 1879 he went to America in an emigrant ship, and there he married. Later in life he settled at Samoa, where he bought a property and where he seemed at one time to be recovering his health. The hope proved illusory, and he died suddenly from the rupture of a blood-vessel in his brain.

Stevenson was always a conscientious craftsman, as careful in the building of his prose as his father had been when constructing a lighthouse. He wrote verse, criticism, commentary and novels, his unfinished novel, *The Master of Ballantrae*, having the makings of a masterpiece. He was a delightful letter-writer, and his adventure story *The Sea Cook* or *Treasure Island*, re-issued in book form under its alternative title, has been well loved ever since in the schoolroom and on the boards of the theatre for the characters of Jim Hawkins, Captain Flint, Long John Silver, blind Pew, and the marooned Ben Gunn. Stevenson had the gift for names as well as for narrative.

One of the best portraits is by Count Nerli (*d.* 1926), and it hangs in Stevenson's native city.

WILDE was the son of an eminent Irish surgeon, and, after being at Trinity College, Dublin, he went to Magdalen College, Oxford, where he became known for aestheticism and eccentricity. He was the subject of caricature in Gilbert and Sullivan's opera *Patience*, produced in 1881, which was in itself a sign of his influence. In the same year he published his first volume of poems.

In 1891 appeared *The Picture of Dorian Gray*, Wilde's only novel; then followed a succession of plays which delighted London audiences and which are constantly and triumphantly revived – *Lady Windermere's Fan*, *A Woman of No Importance*, and *The Importance of Being Ernest*. No comedies equalled them in glitter since the days of Sheridan.

Wilde's later years were tragic. In 1895 he was sentenced to a term of imprisonment for sexual offences, and his name ceased to be heard on respectable lips. While in prison he wrote 'The Ballad of Reading Gaol' and 'De Profundis', showing how his experiences had affected his outlook. This was in fact never as superficial as it may have appeared, for like many writers of wit, he was well aware of the more challenging problems of mankind.

Wilde had faithful admirers abroad, and the sparkling clarity of his prose made him readily translatable. One of the writers well commemorated by the photographer, he is seen at the height of his London success.

GEORGE BERNARD SHAW ('I do not like being George'd,' he once wrote) was born in Dublin. He came to London in 1876 and made a reputation as a music, art and dramatic critic. Feeling deeply about many political and economic questions, he became a member of the Fabian Society, founded in 1884 by Socialists who favoured a policy of harassing tactics to effect reform, rather than attempts at revolutionary action in the Russian style.

Shaw's iconoclasm and his delight in mocking, shocking, scandalising and ridiculing, together with the power of a born humorist to evoke explosive laughter, earned his plays sensational success, which enabled him to use the theatre as a pulpit from which to preach social philosophy. This he also expounded in long prefaces to the printed versions. Shaw wrote over fifty plays, and also social commentary which was exciting to his contemporaries. Since his death, interest in his work has continued.

For all his superficial foolery, Shaw was a fundamentally serious artist who treated every theme he handled freshly, so that in his historical dramas, such as *St Joan*, the scenes are re-enacted as if they happened yesterday.

Augustus John (1878-1961), who painted Hardy, also saw Shaw with perceptive eyes.

JOSEPH CONRAD, whose name at birth was Jósef Teodor Konrad Nalecz Korzeniowski, was born in Poland at a time when his country, which had long been proudly independent, was under Russian rule. His family was distinguished: it had produced soldiers, thinkers and men of letters. His father's dearest wish was to see Poland free.

As a youth, Conrad took service in the French merchant marine, but he soon transferred to that of Great Britain, in whose ships he sailed for nearly twenty years. He rose to command: but before he left the sea he had begun to write. His earlier novels had their setting in far eastern isles and waters which Conrad found inspiring to his imagination.

From the year 1895, when he published *Almayer's Folly*, until the time of his death nearly thirty years later, Conrad produced works of extraordinary range, many, though by no means all, concerned with his earlier calling. He believed his masterpiece to have been *Nostromo*, which appeared in 1904. More popular were *Lord Jim*, and some of his other tales, including *Youth*, *Typhoon*, *The Shadow Line*, and *Heart of Darkness*, the latter a grim story based on his own experience of the Congo.

When Conrad died, he was a major figure on both sides of the Atlantic. Shortly before his death Walter Tittle, an American artist still living, made a study of him in dry-point which is at once characteristic and attractive.

> . . . a line will take us hours maybe;
> Yet if it does not seem a moment's thought,
> Our stitching and unstitching has been naught.

So wrote Yeats of the skill to which he dedicated his life, that of writing verse which would have immediate impact and sustained value. He wrote elsewhere:

'All things can tempt me from this craft of verse. . . .' This expressed not only a mood of exasperation at the toil of creation with which every artist grows familiar, but an urge to take part in politics and affairs which he found irresistible.

William Butler Yeats was born in Dublin, and was educated there and in London. This was significant in the sense that all through his life he was aware both of the particular call of his country, of which in due time he became a Senator, and of the claims of English and indeed of world literature. He studied art for three years, but when still very young adopted writing as his profession. Inspired by the Gaelic Movement, he helped to found Irish literary societies in London and in Ireland itself. He also applied himself to the creation of an Irish National Theatre. The wish was partly fulfilled, with the help of Lady Gregory (1852-1932) and others, when his play *The Countess Cathleen* was performed in Dublin in 1899. The Irish National Theatre Company was formed later, and the Abbey Theatre, which was to become the home of the Irish Players, flourished as their centre.

Yeats's greatest achievement was as a lyric poet. He was a man of intellect and feeling who changed and grew. He was writing better in his last decades than in his youth, and there are few in any epoch of whom that may truthfully be said.

THE interpreter of an Empire which has since dissolved into another pattern – a process which he would have understood – Kipling was born in India, and was educated at the United Services College, Westward Ho! of which he gave a rollicking description, with himself in the character of 'Beetle', in *Stalky and Co.*

He lived in America and elsewhere before settling down at Burwash in Sussex, a county whose history enthralled him. His intention had always been to master different aspects of writing, and in large measure he succeeded. His kinsman, Sir Philip Burne-Jones (1861-1926) shows him as he appeared in 1899 at the height of his fame. A picture of one of his beloved ships of war is above his table, and the portrait catches the spirit of Kipling's craftsman's attitude to letters.

Kipling wrote many books of short stories, the best of which bear comparison even with those of the French masters. He was a prolific writer of verse, some of which has stood the test of time, and at least one of his narratives, *Kim*, gives a pattern of India hard to rival in any other single work. Kipling's children's books, such as *Puck of Pook's Hill* and *The Jungle Book*, show an imaginative understanding of the young, and of animals, which has been valued by successive generations in schoolroom and nursery.

Kipling left an assortment of other writing ranging from topical commentary to military history. No one celebrated the man of action better, or shared his own enjoyment of life more generously.

A PIONEER in science fiction, and a novelist of ability
in the comic tradition, H. G. Wells was the son of a
small tradesman, his mother being for some years house-
keeper at Uppark, a great house on the Sussex Downs to
which he paid eloquent tribute in his *An Experiment in
Autobiography*.

In early life Wells was apprenticed to a draper. He
then became a teacher at Midhurst Grammar School,
later graduating at the Normal School of Science, South
Kensington. By the age of thirty he felt confident
enough of his powers and energy to live by writing.

His novels and stories divide into fantastic and imaginative romances. *The Country of the Blind* contains excellent examples in short story form: there are novels of
character and humour, such as *The History of Mr Polly*:
finally there are discussion novels, such as *The World of
William Clissold* in which everything is subordinated to
ideas, character taking a secondary place. This was the
type of work on which Wells was much engaged towards
the end of his life.

The sweep of history, and the habits and fate of the
mass of mankind fascinated Wells, and led him to write
an *Outline of History*, but in proceeding from the particular to the general he lost something in the process,
though he was following an irresistible attraction. Few
writers have known sections of English society better, or
portrayed them more sympathetically, and Wells added
to other gifts one of prophecy, particularly in the sphere
of war and scientific discovery.

BORN and brought up in the Potteries, which he called in his books the Five Towns – Tunstall, Burslem, Hanley, Stoke-upon-Trent and Longton – Enoch Arnold Bennett launched himself on London in 1893, first as a journalist on *Woman*, and then, from 1900 onward, mainly as a novelist.

Bennett was a craftsman who deliberately wrote pot-boilers and, with infinitely greater pains, a series of realistic novels on which he hoped his reputation would rest, a matter about which he was not mistaken. His principal serious novels were *The Old Wives Tale*, a series relating to the Clayhanger family, and *Riceyman Steps*, one of the best studies of miserliness in fiction, the story of a man who needlessly starves himself to death, and infects his wife with the same passion.

Bennett's journalism was kindly and to the point, and he also wrote a number of successful plays, mainly in collaboration. Very materially minded, he intended from the first to be a worldly success, and in this aim he succeeded so completely that he was dazzled by the benefits which success brought him. He had a bad stammer, but his determination overcame even this handicap.

Walter Tittle, who drew that very different contemporary Joseph Conrad, was equally successful in his rendering of a man who liked to think of himself as a 'card'.

DERIVING from West Country stock, being a member of a family which later found prosperity elsewhere, Galsworthy was educated at Harrow and at New College, Oxford. He was one of the comparatively rare writers always able to follow their bent, thanks to a private income. He had the determination to succeed in his chosen way of life, which was that of novelist and playwright, and in due time he came to be valued abroad almost as much as in his own country. His *Forsyte Saga*, a series of novels in which a sense of property is paramount, was held to represent a fairly typical English upper middle class family, and this is not far from the truth.

In his plays, Galsworthy's purpose was to throw light on dark places, and to try to do so impartially. *Strife*, produced in 1909, one of his earlier stage successes, concerned an industrial dispute, and the succeeding play, *Justice*, had practical effects in ameliorating some of the harshness of the prison system. Among other plays with a social implication were *The Skin Game* and *Loyalties*, the later being a testing of the anti-Semitic prejudices in otherwise fair-minded people.

If some of Galsworthy's themes and their treatment have proved only of passing interest, the portraits in the Forsyte series of novels have value in a more lasting sense. Galsworthy was a conscientious craftsman, and an exceptionally liberal-minded man. As the annalist of a cross-section of society, his work is full enough to give him stature.

GILES LYTTON STRACHEY, who came of a family which had given distinguished service as soldiers and administrators in India and elsewhere, was a leading member of that group of writers and artists whose names are linked with Bloomsbury. Virginia and Leonard Woolf, Clive and Vanessa Bell, Maynard Keynes and E. M. Forster were among his friends. His service to letters was to free biography from stuffing. It had been done before, but seldom with such consistent sparkle.

At Trinity College, Cambridge, Strachey specialised in French, the result being one of the most succinct, swift-flowing and understanding surveys of its kind, *Landmarks in French Literature*. It was his first book, and it appeared in 1912, to be followed six years later, at the end of the first World War, by *Eminent Victorians*. This comprised brief biographies of Cardinal Manning, Florence Nightingale, Arnold of Rugby and General Gordon. They were remarkable for their iconoclasm, and they suited a jaded generation. Strachey described his method as avoiding 'scrupulous narration' and attacking his subject, 'in unexpected places', shooting 'a sudden revealing searchlight into obscure recesses, hitherto undivined'. It was a dangerous system, but it matured, in *Queen Victoria*, into a memorable short study of a very long reign. Strachey's one other sustained work, *Elizabeth and Essex*, was a narrative of the first Elizabeth and her ill-starred favourite.

Strachey inspired one of the best portraits in the entire range of such work, by Henry Lamb(1885-1960).

VIRGINIA WOOLF

1882-1941

VIRGINIA WOOLF was the daughter of Sir Leslie Stephen (1832-1904), eminent as a man of letters and the original of Vernon Whitford ('A Phoebus Apollo turned fasting friar') in Meredith's *The Egoist*. Her mother was Harriet Marian, Thackeray's younger daughter, and she married Leonard Woolf, administrator, writer and publisher, with whom she founded the Hogarth Press.

Virginia Woolf's reputation derives from her novels and, to a lesser degree, from her criticism. Her novels, which include *The Voyage Out*, *Night and Day*, *Mrs Dalloway*, *To the Lighthouse*, and *The Waves*, are tirelessly experimental, and the story, in her hands, tends to become something very different from the mere fictional narrative which contented most of her contemporaries and the larger number of her predecessors. How agonising Virginia Woolf found the labour of composition, of writing and re-writing, is described in *A Writer's Diary*, which appeared after her death.

Virginia Wolf was a practising critic most of her life, one whose illumination equalled her clarity. Her two series, addressed to the Common Reader ('I rejoice to concur with the common reader'), have given as much pleasure as any criticism of this century.

Various artists painted and sculptured Virginia Woolf's sad and lovely face, but the camera also caught the quality of magic she possessed.

ONE of those ceaseless experimenters of which every literature must have practitioners if it is to flourish, James Augustine Aloysius Joyce was born at Rathgar, a suburb of Dublin, and was educated at Jesuit Colleges. Dissatisfied with the intellectual atmosphere of Ireland, Joyce left his home in 1902 and spent most of the rest of his life on the Continent, chiefly in Trieste, Zurich and Paris, contending with poverty, suffering latterly from severe eye trouble, and achieving recognition comparatively late in life.

In *Dubliners* and *Portrait of the Artist as a Young Man*, Joyce showed that he could write powerfully within normal conventions, but it was not until the appearance of *Ulysses* that the full measure of his strength was apparent. *Ulysses* narrates a single day's life, actions and thoughts microscopically revealed, of two middle-class Irishmen, Leopold Bloom and Stephen Dedalus, dwellers in Dublin. It seemed to add a new dimension to the novel at a time (1922) when that art form needed an injection of new life. Joyce's later work, particularly *Finnegan's Wake*, carried experiment in language and idea as far as it could reasonably be taken, and sometimes beyond; but by extending the boundaries of fiction Joyce performed a signal service. Some of his work may remain little more than a curiosity, but his single-minded aim of originality produced its effect upon a whole generation. Jacques-Emile Blanche (1862-1942) painted Joyce in 1935.

D. H. LAWRENCE was a Nottinghamshire miner's son, and the fact is significant not merely because, in novels such as *Sons and Lovers* (1913) and *Women in Love* (1921) he showed that he understood his environment as few have done, but because he had the fearless freedom of spirit which traditionally belongs to a mining community.

For some years Lawrence taught in elementary schools; he then began a life of writing and wandering, much helped by the understanding companionship of his wife. His conscious zest for life was increasingly heightened by the knowledge that his own was likely to be short, and this proved to be so, for he died of consumption at Vence at the age of forty-five.

Lawrence was always in rebellion against what he considered to be inhibiting conventions. Everything he wrote, his novels, stories, poems and travel books, were written with passionate absorption, and he believed that western man had warped his instincts by over-cultivating his intellect. Long before he achieved posthumous notoriety through the general publication of one of his least remarkable books, *Lady Chatterley's Lover* (1928), which had originally appeared either abroad or in expurgated form, he had been recognised as one of the most dynamic personalities which had ever used fiction as a vehicle for ideas. Lawrence could be angry, crude, ignorant, and his translation into a latter-day saint and prophet has its ironies, but he affected the English novel deeply and for its lasting good.

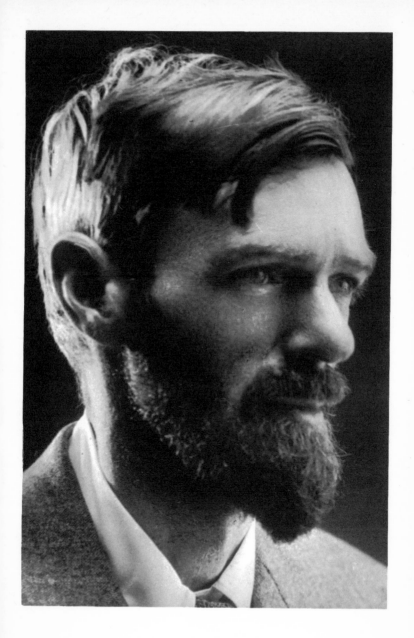

WILFRED OWEN was killed at the age of twenty-five, trying to get his men across the Sambre Canal, just a week before the Armistice of 11 November 1918 put an end to the interminable slaughter of the first World War.

Born at Oswestry, educated at Birkenhead, the opening of the war found him tutoring in France, where he stayed until he joined up. His career as a soldier was distinguished, but throughout the years of fighting he was composing poetry – the poetry of agonised protest. He had begun writing before war broke out, with encouragement from Laurent Tailhade.

Slender as his poems bulk, they speak for a generation. They are a magnificent and terrible answer to any who attempt – from the safety of rear areas or any other vantage point – to glorify war.

> What passing-bells for those who die as cattle?
> Only the monstrous anger of the guns.

Before he died, Owen's qualities were recognised by those who best could value them – by such men as Siegfried Sassoon and Edward Blunden, who had shared the agonies of France and Flanders in the front line. Had Owen lived, his craftsmanship would have developed, for he was an eager experimenter: as it is, his memorial is eloquent.

Eric Hugh Blair, who wrote under the name of George Orwell, was born in India and was educated at Eton. He spent some years as an administrator in Burma, an experience of which he wrote in *Burmese Days* and *Shooting an Elephant*, then, returning to Europe, he endured the miseries and frustrations of being down and out in Paris and London, which he described graphically.

Always politically conscious, Orwell fought against Franco in the Spanish Civil War, during which he was wounded. In the later years of his short life, he wrote with increasing effect upon subjects which engrossed his generation, and in particular on the monolithic State.

The book which brought Orwell fame was *Animal Farm*, a satire classical in form and flawless in execution. Never was the progress of the devouring State so ruthlessly, so wittily exposed, and the pace and clarity of the narrative were reminiscent of Swift. His horrifying novel, *Nineteen Eighty-Four*, published the year before he died, foreshadowed the kind of society which might pervade England if the doctrinaire and the power-maniac had their way.

Orwell's strength was in depicting actualities, and in the imagination which he brought to themes about which he felt deeply. If his prophecies come true, we have been warned. If they do not, they will be enjoyed because they are expressed in a prose which is as persuasive as Cobbett's. Orwell loved political freedom, sympathised passionately with the under-dog, and was incapable, in his writing, of the sly attitude. He could be wrong. He could not be dishonest.

INDEX
OF SUBJECTS AND ARTISTS